AMERICA'S NEEDLESS WARS

AMERICA'S NEEDLESS WARS

CAUTIONARY TALES OF US
INVOLVEMENT IN THE PHILIPPINES,
VIETNAM, AND IRAQ

DAVID R. CONTOSTA

Prometheus Books

59 John Glenn Drive
Amherst, New York 14228

Published 2017 by Prometheus Books

Top right and bottom cover image © Getty Images
Cover design by Liz Mills
Cover design © Prometheus Books

Inquiries should be addressed to
Prometheus Books
59 John Glenn Drive
Amherst, New York 14228
VOICE: 716–691–0133
FAX: 716–691–0137
WWW.PROMETHEUSBOOKS.COM

21 20 19 18 17   5 4 3 2 1

Library of Congress Cataloging-in-Publication Data Pending

Printed in the United States of America

In memory of Virginia Fetters,
our tenth-grade English teacher in Lancaster, Ohio,
who taught us to write and to question.

CONTENTS

ACKNOWLEDGMENTS

I am again grateful to the many friends, colleagues, and family members who discussed this project with me and gave both encouragement and support. I am especially indebted to fellow faculty members here at Chestnut Hill College, particularly Lorraine Coons, Jacki Reich, Anne Pluta, and Kimberly Leahy. I also want to thank the college for granting me a sabbatical and several course releases. Cheering me on were President Carol Jean Vale, SSJ; Academic Dean Cecelia Cavanaugh, SSJ; and Vice President for Academic Affairs Wolfgang Natter. I also bounced ideas off William Walker, a former academic administrator here at the college, a historian in his own right, and a friend of many years. And as always, I am thankful for the never-failing assistance of the staff of the college's Logue Library.

A series of lectures about this book, then in manuscript form, that I delivered at Pyeongtaek University in South Korea helped me to sharpen my thoughts and conclusions as I was making final revisions. These lectures would not have been possible without my excellent interpreter and translator, Dr. Jeongwoo Han. I especially benefited from my discussions with Dr. Nam Kim of Pyeongtaek's Department of American Studies about a variety of diplomatic and foreign policy issues. The hospitality showered on me at Pyeongtaek was unparalleled in my experience. I shall never forget the special kindnesses of University President Dr. Ki Hung Cho, Director of Development Dr. Jung Bok Ha, and Director of External Affairs Kyle Jung.

My walking partners and dear friends, Stan and Leslie Finegold, patiently listened to me spout off about my writing as we made one turn after another around Victory Fields at Plymouth-Whitemarsh High School in Lafayette Hill, Pennsylvania, where we live, and they made some very sound suggestions. And once again, my three daughters, Nicole, Alexandra, and Jessica, and my two sons, David and John, had to hear Dad give impromptu perorations about his latest scholarly passion.

I am delighted once again to be working with Steven L. Mitchell, vice president and editor in chief of Prometheus Books. Members of the Prometheus team have also assisted me at every turn, including Jake Bonar, Jeffrey Curry, Hanna Etu, Mark Hall, Jill Maxick, Lisa Michalski, Lynette Nisbet, Liz Mills, Amy Vigrass, and Cheryl Quimba. In addition, my copyeditor, Jacqueline May Parkison, did a masterful job of putting the manuscript into final form.

CHAPTER 1

INTRODUCTION

"Great is the guilt of an unnecessary war."
—John Adams

W hen I was growing up during the Cold War, I had no doubt God was on America's side. The church our family attended proclaimed this belief with an American flag prominently displayed up front on one side of the sanctuary, with a second flag featuring the Christian cross on the other side. As a member of the Boy Scouts of America, I could earn what was called the "God and Country" award.

Then, as a university student, I learned that believing God was on America's side was nothing new: The English Puritans, who settled Boston and later the rest of New England, believed God had made them a second chosen people and had sent them to the New World to save the corrupt and decadent Old World. For them, Boston was a new Jerusalem and a new Israel—a new Promised Land. This belief eventually seeped out of New England to much of the rest of America and is still held by many citizens today.

Sometime during college, I shed my belief that God favored Americans above all other people, but I did come to share the principal thoughts of our Founding Fathers during and after the American Revolution. Men like Thomas Jefferson, Benjamin Franklin, and John Adams were sons of the eighteenth-century Enlightenment. They believed that, through reason and experience, Americans could establish a political system and way of life that might save them from the moral stains of that hopeless Old World across the Atlantic.

The Great Seal of the United States says it all; the reverse side includes both religious and secular sentiments about what has come to be called American exceptionalism. One can also find these sentiments on the green side of the American $1 bill: *Annuit coeptis*, Latin meaning "He has favored our undertakings," and *Novus ordo seclorum*, Latin meaning "A new order of the ages."

As I continued to study and then teach American history, I found myself becoming something of a disappointed idealist. I really wanted my country to represent "A new order of the ages"—one that would not repeat the failings of the Old World—and that meant, among other things, not fighting needless wars. Much later, it struck me that during one long modern lifetime of 105 years, from 1898 to 2003, the United States initiated three wholly needless wars—in the Philippines, in Vietnam, and in Iraq.

Altogether, nearly sixty-seven thousand Americans lost their lives in these needless conflicts, and the death toll for those on the other sides was at least two million. Then there were the millions of hideous wounds, the inestimable emotional and psychological suffering, and the mourning of countless families. Very disturbing also were the atrocities committed on all sides, including those carried out by American soldiers in the Philippines, Vietnam, and Iraq that led to questions about our country's moral standing in the world.

I do not mean to say that I am a pacifist, since I believe some wars are unavoidable and must be fought. After all, my father and the fathers of many schoolmates and friends fought a terrible conflict to free suffering millions on several continents. As children, we saw these World War II veterans march quietly in the annual Memorial Day parade, up one of the main streets of town to the local cemetery on the hill, where there was a moving ceremony, complete with the playing of taps. During my parents' childhoods, there had still been a few ancient veterans of the Civil War in the parade, forced by infirmities to ride in open cars. They had fought desperate battles, we learned, to save the Union and free the slaves.

The wars in the Philippines, Vietnam, and Iraq were different. They were different because true national security was not at stake. None of these countries posed a grave threat to the United States—or even came close to doing so. The Philippines at the end of the nineteenth century was an underdeveloped country located halfway around the world from the United States and had no capacity whatsoever to harm the American nation. Even the argument that other powers might take over these islands to the detriment of American economic interests made no rational sense, given that the United States could well have protected Philippine independence after defeating the Spanish colonial government there. Besides that, the provisional Philippine government initially welcomed American support and reached out the hand of friendship to the United States.

Nor, half a century later, did a third-world country like Vietnam pose a serious threat to American security, unless one believed its bid for independence at the end of World War II was part of a worldwide communist conspiracy. In fact, the indigenous postwar government of Vietnam sought American friendship and support, much as the Filipinos had done two generations earlier. Instead, the United States backed France in its efforts to reconquer its former Southeast Asian colonies, and after France was defeated, it continued to fight against Vietnam's ever-tenacious struggle to be free of foreign rule. And when the United States lost the war in Vietnam three decades later, predictions that Communism would spread from the Indo-Chinese peninsula far and wide turned out to be false.

In the early twenty-first century, Iraq by no means posed an existential threat to the United States. Contrary to claims by the George W. Bush administration, Iraq had nothing to do with the terrorist attacks on the United States on September 11, 2001. Nor, as the administration also claimed, did Iraq have any "weapons of mass destruction." And instead of bolstering the nation's security, the invasion of Iraq in 2003 so destabilized the country that it became a serious liability to the United States, the entire Middle East, and beyond.

All three wars violated a core principle of what is known as "just war theory," a body of well-established norms that can be traced back 1,600 years to Saint Augustine of Hippo. More modern understandings of just war reach back about three centuries and have become embedded in international law, such as the Charter of the United Nations and the various Geneva conventions. Central to all these norms are the concepts of "necessity" and "last resort." Michael Walzer, in his highly regarded book *Just and Unjust Wars*, encompasses these two requirements under his definition of "supreme emergency."[1] For a supreme emergency to exist, Walzer writes, the danger to the country must be eminent and "of an unusual and horrifying kind," conditions that nations clearly faced with German aggression in World War II.[2]

It is clear from the evidence that the wars in the Philippines, Vietnam, and Iraq do not meet the criteria of supreme emergencies—or even moderate emergencies—that would give the United States no alternative but to resort to war. How, then, to explain why presidents and their supporters decided to take the country to war in these three cases? By and large, the answer is that the decision makers, namely presidents and their political allies, acted out of ignorance, arrogance, and unreasoning fears, combined with partisan gamesmanship and the failure of media to inform the public accurately about the drive to war and its possible consequences.

Ignorance, arrogance, and fear can be seen as an intertwined and self-reinforcing triad. Ignorance of the history, culture, and conditions of other people and nations contributes directly to suspicion and fear of them as unknown and possibly hostile entities. Ignorance also feeds arrogance, since it encourages simplistic claims that the realities of a situation are very simple and that the task of defeating any enemies will be easy and straightforward. Arrogance and fear also go hand in hand, especially when leaders exaggerate fears and then make arrogant promises that they and they alone know how to vanquish the source of those fears. Such leaders resemble old-time preachers who conjured up horrific images of evil and then promised only they could offer deliverance.

For instance, ignorance (sometimes willful) of the people, history, and customs of the Philippines, Vietnam, and Iraq led to costly and serious miscalculations about whether and how local populations would likely react to forceful American intrusions. Arrogance led presidents and their advisors to believe their country could work its will anywhere in the world regardless of circumstances—that, for instance, the United States could implant democracy in places like Iraq, where it had never existed and where conditions would not be favorable to it at any time in the near future. Irrational fear caused leaders to exaggerate threats to national security and prevented them from adopting well-thought-out, proportional solutions. Nowhere was this sort of fear more debilitating than in the false belief that a tenacious Vietnamese nationalism was really part of a worldwide Communist conspiracy.

Partisan politics also have played a role in limiting or distorting rational debate over war policy. In 1898, Democrats, as well as members of President McKinley's own Republican Party, heaped unrelenting abuse on the president because he was a reluctant warrior, going so far as to call him an unmanly coward. The several presidents, beginning with Truman, who got the nation embroiled in Vietnam constantly feared the political opposition would accuse them of being "soft on Communism" if they did not keep Vietnam from falling into Communist hands, despite the fact that the civil war in Vietnam was mostly about nationalism and self-determination. And in the aftermath of the attacks on the United States on September 11, 2001, many politicians feared questioning the march to war with Iraq would be used to accuse them of being against the "War on Terror," even though Iraq and its leader, Saddam Hussein, had nothing whatsoever to do with the 9/11 attacks.

Unfortunately, the media, often referred to as the "fourth branch of government," largely failed to do their job of informing the American people accurately about the arguments for and against war. In the late 1890s, many newspapers actually fanned the flames for war with Spain, which in turn fomented the United States–Philippines conflict. In the long lead-up to the Vietnam tragedy, which began almost immediately after World War II, the media asked few questions about American involvement in Southeast Asia. And between 2001 and 2003, during the run-up to the war in Iraq, the media were, for the most part, uncritical. Only when these three wars began to go badly did various news outlets partly redeem themselves by questioning the decision for war and attempting to give a more accurate picture of how the conflict was unfolding. The reasons for the media's failure were these: positive reporting on demands for war attracted readers, listeners, and viewers; and media executives did not want to be out of step with public opinion or find themselves accused of insufficient patriotism. Put more simply, failure to fall in line with calls for war might well be bad for business.

All three wars discussed below also illustrate that it is much easier to start a war than to end it. Nations at war will usually continue to fight long after defeat is obvious or inevitable, even if it means doing calamitous injury to their own people. And no matter what leaders predict, wars invariably spin out of control, take on lives of their own, and have unintended consequences, which often must be justified with contorted or false explanations of the reasons for initiating war—and then continuing it. For example, the United States went to war in 1898 to free the Cuban people from Spanish rule and then, only months later, fought a brutal war to deny Filipinos their independence. In Vietnam, the United States waged a conflict allegedly to stop Communist aggression but instead became trapped in a civil war for independence with no end in sight. The war in Iraq was officially begun to bring about "regime change," with predictions that American forces would be welcomed as liberators. Instead, Iraq descended into anarchy and sectarian warfare.

No matter how disastrous these wars became, the presidents who presided over them vowed to continue the fighting no matter what. To end these wars short of victory would have led to charges that the presidents and their supporters at best were guilty of very bad judgment and at worst had expended large numbers of lives unnecessarily. Presidents, especially, are unwilling to make such devastating admissions, which would be tantamount to political suicide. As the Prussian general and military theorist Carl von Clausewitz wrote (in italics) nearly two centuries ago, *"War is only a branch of political activity; . . . it is in no sense autonomous."*[3]

Few historians or other analysts have made significant comparisons among the three wars discussed here. During the Iraq conflict, there was some mention of the fact that American interrogators had used waterboarding, or a form of torture similar to it, in both the Philippines and Iraq. The My Lai massacre in Vietnam led to some references to similar massacres in the Philippines. More comparisons have been made between ill-conceived, open-ended military commitments in both Vietnam and Iraq. And some fragmentary comments have surfaced about how Americans faced irregular (guerrilla) forces in all three places. But there has been no thoroughgoing attempt to examine American wars in the Philippines, Vietnam, and Iraq as parts of a pattern of needless, elective conflicts.

One might ask what good could result from reexamining and comparing these three wars. One might even say that the Philippine War took place at a "bad old time" in American history—at a time before those in power had gained the knowledge and sophistication to deal more adeptly with war and foreign affairs. Unfortunately, several generations of leaders since then have repeated the mistakes of that earlier time. So the answer is that these three wars can serve as cautionary tales. Of course, history does not repeat itself exactly, but, as Mark Twain put it, "history . . . does rhyme." All of us, individuals as well as whole societies, do learn—or should learn—from the rhythms of the past as a basis for survival and progress in the present and future.

This book is not a criticism of the millions of brave and honorable men and women who have served in our armed forces. Nor does it accuse the relevant decision makers of evil intentions—of being leaders who wished to see thousands of people killed and maimed. Rather, this book argues that presidents, legislators, and opinion makers, acting through ignorance, arrogance, unreasoning fear, and political gamesmanship, have too often sent the nation's sons and daughters to fight needless wars that have cost unnecessary lives and stained the nation's reputation.

This book is offered as an inquiry into why the United States would fight these three needless wars. In the process, I have sifted through official hearings, media investigations, public documents, and numerous histories, including the memoirs of those who supported or opposed the various marches to war and their conduct. I have done so in hopes that lessons might emerge for future generations and decision makers, thereby avoiding further stains on the fabric of American life.

CHAPTER 2
CUBAN PROLOGUE

"We are face to face with a strange destiny. The taste of Empire is in the mouth of the people even as the taste of blood in the jungle. . . ."
—*Washington Post* editorial

The American conquest of the Philippine Islands, then a Spanish colony for some three centuries, grew out of a war between the United States and Spain that had started halfway around the world in a dispute over Cuba. In 1898, those beating the drums for war with Spain gave no thought to the possibility of a long and bloody aftermath in the Philippines—an aftermath that would be undertaken in almost total ignorance of the history and culture of the islands—or the long-term consequences of conquering this distant archipelago. Such ignorance, combined with an arrogant assertion of white Anglo-Saxon superiority, led the United States into a brutal and unnecessary war of conquest. The deadly triangle of ignorance, arrogance, and fear was completed by the irrational worry that if the United States did not take the Philippines, another great power could not be prevented from doing so and thus depriving the American people of their supposedly rightful place in Asia. Added to this mix were political machinations that stood in the way of clear and accurate analysis, along with strident claims that the United States needed a war to preserve its manhood and save its people from lives of sloth and ease. Finally, the wildly irresponsible reporting of the media of the day fanned the flames of war.

Many cultural and economic factors also figured in the coming of the Spanish-American War and its imperial aftermath. The rapid industrial growth of the United States in the decades after the Civil War was making it the wealthiest and most productive country on earth. Even so, a deep economic depression beginning in 1893 caused many leaders to claim the economic crisis had resulted from an industrial overproduction that only new overseas markets could absorb. In the words of US senator Albert J. Beveridge of Indiana, speaking in early 1897, "American factories are making more than the American people can use; American soil is producing more than they can consume. Fate has written our policy for us; the trade of the world must and shall be ours."[1] In fact, fairer wages for workers would have been a far better and safer way to boost demand for goods in the home market.[2]

In addition, a belief was emerging in some quarters that to become a great world power, the United States needed to join the imperial club or risk being left behind. This was a sentiment shared by big navy advocates, who insisted expanding foreign trade required the United States to build a modern, world-class navy. The most important and effective advocate for enhanced naval power was naval captain Alfred Thayer Mahan, who was a faculty member (and later president) of the US Naval War College. Mahan taught and wrote about naval history with an emphasis on the connection between sea power and the status of nations on the world stage. His most influential book was *The Influence of Sea Power upon History*, published in 1890. Throughout history, Mahan asserted, the key to power, wealth, and greatness was control of the seas. His book had a profound influence on US foreign policy and was widely admired in Britain as well as among naval planners and policy personnel in Germany and Japan. Mahan's greatest booster in the United States was future president Theodore Roosevelt, who would use Mahan's ideas to push for a larger and more up-to-date American navy.

Mahan also supported the revival of American manifest destiny, a concept that had first appeared, at least explicitly, a half century before at the approach of war between the United States and Mexico. Now it would be used to advocate for an overseas American empire. Although the primary arguments for it concerned economic and strategic needs, American manifest destiny also contained racist elements. Central to these racial arguments was the so-called Anglo-Saxon myth (also known as the Teutonic myth, at least before World

War I and the demonization of Germany). The myth went somewhat as follows: The three most powerful countries in the world in the late nineteenth century were Germany, Great Britain, and the United States. This was surely a matter of racial superiority (rather than fortuitous circumstances such as location, natural resources, cultural evolution, and timing). Linguists pointed out the Germanic roots of the English language. Historians focused on the fact that the Angles and Saxons (that is, Germanic tribes) had invaded England from the mid-fifth through the early seventh centuries and that some of their descendants went to Britain's North American colonies—including the future United States—centuries later.

Associated with and reinforcing the Anglo-Saxon myth was social Darwinism with the concept of "survival of the fittest." This phrase was actually coined by Englishman Herbert Spencer, whose methods and views drew considerable scorn from Charles Darwin. In truth, Darwin asserted in his writings about human evolution that community and cooperation were far more important in the development of civilization than the sort of ruthless competition espoused by imperialists and laissez-faire economists. As Darwin himself pointed out, making comparisons between biology and culture amounted to false analogies and pseudoscience. In this sense, the term *social Darwinism* blames Darwin unfairly for views that he did not hold and that should not have been used to justify imperial conquests. *Social evolution* would be a more accurate term, but *social Darwinism* has become so firmly implanted that it is unlikely to be discarded.[3]

Typical of those Americans who lauded American and Anglo-Saxon superiority was John W. Burgess, a law professor and political scientist at Columbia University. According to him, the Teutonic (including Anglo-Saxon) nations were "peculiarly endowed with the capacity for establishing national states, and . . . especially called to that work; and therefore . . . they are entrusted, in the general economy of history, with the mission of conducting the political civilization of the modern word."[4] Another advocate was the Reverend Josiah Strong, who asked in his very popular 1885 tract *Our Country*, "Does it not look as if God were not only preparing in our Anglo-Saxon civilization the die with which to stamp the peoples of the earth, but as if He were massing behind that die the mighty power with which to press it?"[5] According to Strong, both God and evolution had formed the Anglo-Saxon peoples, and especially those who had populated the United States, into a superior people with the right to dominate the world.

On the eve of the Spanish-American War, an editorial in the *Washington Post* declared that the country was more than ready to fulfill its imperial destiny:

> A new consciousness seems to have come upon us—the consciousness of strength—and with it a new appetite, the yearning to show our strength. . . . Ambition, interest, land hunger, pride, the mere joy of fighting, whatever it may be, we are animated by a new sensation. We are face to face with a strange destiny. The taste of Empire is in the mouth of the people even as the taste of blood in the jungle . . .[6]

In extolling the sheer joy of fighting, the *Post* was tapping into a growing belief that American prosperity and love of money were undermining the country's ideal of self-sacrifice, even though this idea was at odds with those who extolled empire for economic reasons. However contradictory, for many veterans of the Civil War—who had conveniently forgotten the very real horrors of that conflict—war was a noble experience in which soldiers could test their manhood and lift themselves out of narrow materialism and complacency. As Oliver Wendell Holmes, a veteran of the Civil War who was soon to become a celebrated Supreme Court justice, proclaimed, the men who fought that conflict were fortunate in their youths to have had their "hearts touched by fire."[7]

Not all politicians who served in the 1890s agreed with such sentiments. One opponent was President Grover Cleveland, who was an outspoken anti-imperialist during his nonconsecutive presidencies (1885–89 and 1893–97) and who remained a fervent anti-imperialist during and after the Spanish-American War. In 1895, when the latest in a series of rebellions against the Spanish broke out in Cuba, Cleveland believed that continued Spanish control of the island would be the best way to maintain the status quo in the Caribbean. Unlike those who wanted the United States to intervene in Cuba, Cleveland refused to equate the Cuban rebels with the American militiamen at Lexington and Concord and believed the rebels were incapable of forming a stable government to rule the island. On the contrary, he thought, an independent Cuba would be unstable and invite other European powers to exploit the island's weaknesses to gain a foothold in the Caribbean. He therefore proclaimed American neutrality toward Cuba and declined to recognize the belligerency of the rebels.

Another opponent of Cuban involvement was the Speaker of the House of Representatives, Thomas B. Reed, who ruled the House with such an iron hand that he was known as "Czar Reed." He was suspicious of the human tendency to glorify war and did not share the Civil War nostalgia felt by so many, especially those who had been too young to participate. Nor did he believe the United States should be playing world police, since there was plenty of misery at home that needed attention, including economic cycles of boom and bust, a growing divide between rich and poor, and increasing violence against African Americans. A war abroad would only take attention away from these serious domestic problems. Furthermore, Reed thought heavy spending on weapons might well lead to unnecessary conflict caused by an arrogant belief that the United States could easily defeat any opponent. In early 1896, Reed kept the House from voting to recognize the belligerency of the Cuban rebels. A year later, in February 1897, he did not stand in the way of a similar resolution (which had already passed the Senate) because he knew President Cleveland would ignore it in the waning days of his administration.[8]

Cleveland's successor, William McKinley, inherited the Cuban problem when he took office in March 1897. At first, McKinley hoped to stay out of the Cuban imbroglio, vowing there would be "no jingo nonsense" (that is, belligerent foreign policy) in his administration. Just before taking the oath of office, McKinley told the outgoing President Cleveland that he would be the happiest man in the world if he could escape the "terrible calamity" of war.[9] In his inaugural address, McKinley stressed his wish to avoid armed conflict: "We want no wars of conquest; we must avoid the temptation of territorial aggression. War should never be entered upon until every agency of peace has failed; peace is preferable to war in almost every contingency."[10] In other words, war should be a very last resort.

Because he wanted to avoid war if at all possible, the new president had hesitated to appoint Theodore Roosevelt as assistant secretary of the navy "for fear [he would] want to fight somebody at once," in the words of Roosevelt's close friend Henry Cabot Lodge.[11] At first, Roosevelt guarded his words, but he could not contain himself for long, and on June 2, 1897, he gave himself away in a speech to the US Naval War College. As one might expect in an address to such an audience, he called for building up the navy. He rejected any assertions that doing so would invite war but claimed that if it did, war would be a very good thing for the country: "All the great, masterful races have been fighting races," he said, "and the minute that a race loses the hard fighting virtues, then . . . it has lost its proud right to stand as the equal to the best." He added, "Cowardice in a race, as in an individual, is the unpardonable sin." And nothing could surpass victory in war: "No triumph of peace is so great as the supreme triumphs of war. . . . It may be that at some time in the dim future of the [human] race the need for war will vanish; but that time is ages distant." Winding up his speech, he warned against the dangers of prosperity and ease: "There are higher things in this life than the soft and easy enjoyment of material comfort. It is through strife, or the readiness for strife, that a nation must win greatness." If the need arose, the nation must be willing "to stake everything on the supreme arbitrament [*sic*] of war, and to pour out its blood, its treasure, and its tears like water, rather than submit to the loss of honor and renown."[12] He used the word *war* no fewer than sixty-two times in the course of the speech.

McKinley, in a very different frame of mind from Roosevelt, offered in December 1897 to mediate between Spain and the rebels, but the Spanish absolutely refused to consider granting independence to Cuba, and the rebels refused to entertain anything but full independence. In fact, McKinley's offer of intervention may have encouraged the rebels to fight on, and its rejection may have inflamed American public opinion against Spain and heightened demands for the United States to use force.

Since taking office, McKinley had been handicapped by serious ignorance about foreign affairs. American ministers and consuls seldom wrote dispatches back to the State Department about what they observed from their foreign posts, and the State Department itself was short-staffed and ill equipped to digest and convey any information that did arrive. Into this vacuum stepped the popular press of the day, knowing full well that both politicians and the public relied heavily on newspaper reports and editorials about what was happening in the world. Publishers also knew sensational stories with a moral twist, often laced with a convenient disregard for the facts, would help boost circulation.[13]

The so-called yellow press, a shorthand label for the sensational newspapers of the day, which included William Randolph Hearst's *New York Journal* and Joseph Pulitzer's *New York World*, fanned the flames with lurid accounts of Spanish atrocities in Cuba. Some of these were true, some were exaggerated, and some were entirely fabricated. In fact, both the Spanish authorities and the rebels were guilty of terrible atrocities, but the newspapers ignored most of the rebels' deeds and focused on the Spanish. Hearst supposedly told Frederick Remington, then an artist on his staff, "You furnish the pictures and I'll furnish the war."[14] Whether or not the directive came from Hearst himself, Remington obliged with an illustration showing three Spanish men looking on lustfully as they strip-search an attractive, young American woman, who is entirely nude in the image and shown from her attractive backside. The woman had been accused of carrying messages from the Cuban rebels to their junta in New York, but, in reality, her search had been conducted by a (female) matron—not a group of men.[15] Neither Hearst nor other publishers were at all concerned that inflaming public opinion could lead to war. In fact, war was exactly what they wanted, since it would greatly boost circulation.

Two events occurred in February 1898 that gave the newspapers unlimited opportunities for sensational reporting and arousing war fever. One was a private letter by the Spanish minister to Washington, Enrique Dupuy de Lôme. Commenting on the president's recent annual message to Congress, de Lôme wrote, "McKinley's message I regard as bad. . . . It shows once more what McKinley is: weak and catering to the rabble, and, besides, a low politician, who desires to leave a door open to me and to stand well with the jingoes of his party."[16] There was some truth to de Lôme's comments. McKinley was truly in a tight spot. He sincerely wanted to avoid war but was being demanded to use force by the press and wide segments of the public. The rebels managed to steal the de Lôme letter and sent it to the *New York Journal*, which published it on February 9. In a large headline, the rival *New York World* cried that the de Lôme letter was the "WORST INSULT TO THE UNITED STATES IN ITS HISTORY." The revelation triggered widespread public fury, as well as anger among many in government.

Just six days later, on February 15, with outrage over the de Lôme letter still fresh, the USS *Maine* exploded in Havana Harbor, killing 262 Americans. The battleship had been sent to Havana to protect and, if necessary, evacuate Americans in Cuba. The newspapers and the public immediately blamed the explosion on a Spanish torpedo. Assistant Secretary of the Navy Theodore Roosevelt insisted to Congress that the *Maine* was sunk by "an act of dirty treachery on the part of the Spaniards."[17] All over the country, people chanted the phrase, "Remember the *Maine*, to hell with Spain." Meanwhile, hoping to avoid war, Spain removed de Lôme from his post. Spanish authorities in Cuba had begged the United States not to send the *Maine* to Havana, fearing some incident might result. The Spanish helped rescue and care for those injured on the *Maine*, and they allowed an American naval investigation team to come down to Havana. The results of the inquiry were inconclusive: the court of inquiry concluded the ship had been deliberately sunk by a submerged mine, but they could not assign any blame for it. Common sense would have suggested that the Spanish, who did not want a war with the United States they knew they would lose, would not have blown up the ship. If any agents were responsible, it was more likely the rebels, who wanted American help in winning their independence. Most naval experts today believe the explosion was caused when a fire in one of the coal bunkers ignited the ship's powder magazine and set off a massive internal explosion. In fact, this was the conclusion drawn by Spanish authorities, who had undertaken an independent investigation of the disaster.

Also doubting Spanish culpability at the time was Philip Alger, the leading authority on explosive naval ordinance and a professor at the US Naval Academy. The day after the *Maine* sunk, Alger shared his doubts with the *Washington Star*: "No torpedo such as is known in modern warfare," he told the newspaper, "can of itself cause an explosion as powerful as that which destroyed the *Maine*." He added, "We know of no instances where the explosion of a torpedo or mine under a ship's bottom has exploded the [gunpowder] magazine within." The most plausible cause of the sinking, Alger believed, was a spontaneous fire in the coal bunker of the ship, which directly abutted the magazine and was separated from it only by a steel bulkhead—a hazard that was well known from other ships of similar design.[18] Tellingly, Alger was not selected to serve on the court of inquiry established to investigate the *Maine*.

Theodore Roosevelt, based on knowledge gained as assistant secretary of the navy, also knew about the danger of internal explosions in ships with coal bunkers placed next to power magazines.[19] But Roosevelt, who was determined to have his war, was not about to use this information to dampen cries for revenge against Spain. (Such insistence on Spanish culpability was not unlike the US attitude toward Iraq a century later in the aftermath of the 9/11 terror attacks.)

In contrast with Roosevelt, President McKinley, who still hoped for peace, refrained from speaking out about the *Maine*. Just a week after the sinking, he gave a speech at the University of Pennsylvania for George Washington's birthday. In it, he recalled for his audience Washington's cautious advice for dealing with other countries: "Observe good faith and justice toward all nations; cultivate peace and harmony with all."[20]

Roosevelt was furious the president had not denounced Spain or called for war in his speech. Two days later, on February 25—a day Secretary of the Navy John D. Long was out of town—Assistant Secretary Roosevelt cabled Admiral George Dewey, commander of the US Asian fleet, to steam to Manila, the capital of the Philippines, and take the city as soon as there was a declaration of war. In fact, the navy had anticipated such an action as early as June 1896, when plans called for destroying the Spanish Pacific fleet in case of war with Spain so the ships could not be sent to join their Atlantic naval forces. Furthermore, demolishing Spain's naval assets in the Pacific could be used as bargaining leverage in any peace treaty. Still, when

Long learned what Roosevelt had done, the irritated secretary of the navy wrote, "During my short absence I find that Roosevelt, in his precipitate way, has come very near causing more of an explosion than happened to the *Maine*. . . . The very devil seemed to possess him yesterday afternoon."[21] Yet Long did not countermand the order because it was very much in line with preexisting naval war plans; nor did President McKinley. In addition to his orders to Dewey, Roosevelt had also been advocating in private correspondence for months that the United States seize and occupy Manila in case of war.[22]

On March 25, McKinley reluctantly sent Spain an ultimatum demanding an immediate armistice and the granting of Cuban independence. The Spanish government made great efforts to avoid war. They promised autonomy to Cuba, though it was clear the rebels would accept nothing short of total independence. If reason had prevailed, Spain would have admitted the cause was hopeless and the obvious thing to do was to give up and let Cuba go. But such a decision would have spelled political suicide for the ruling party in Spain and may well have resulted in the overthrow of the Spanish monarchy, then under Queen Regent Maria Cristina. These political considerations, along with a strong sense of national honor, required that Spain fight in the face of sure defeat.

Even after his ultimatum, McKinley still hoped to prevent war. "I have been through one war," he said, making reference to his Civil War service. "I have seen the dead piled up, and I do not want to see another."[23] As a staff officer in the Union Army, he had not experienced actual combat and had not come away from the war with a feeling of exaltation or an enhanced sense of manhood. But the political pressure and ridicule from the press put him into a difficult position. Roosevelt declared that the president invited national humiliation by refusing to fight; he supposedly declared in a private letter that McKinley had "no more backbone than a chocolate éclair."[24] The *Washington Post* questioned McKinley's manhood, adding that "a weak or vacillating policy would mean the overwhelming defeat of the Republican party and everlasting repudiation of the administration."[25] Hearst's *New York Journal* printed a cartoon showing the president as a woman wearing a bonnet and apron, and the *Chicago Tribune* featured a cartoon of him as a coward holding out the white feather of surrender. Republican strategists worried the Democrats would soon be campaigning under the slogan "Cuba Libre" as a means of discrediting McKinley and his party.[26]

Yet given McKinley's great popularity, he arguably could have mounted a campaign for patience while continuing to pursue a diplomatic solution. However, to do so, he would have had to spend the previous year building a public case against going to war with Spain. Unfortunately, throughout his public life, McKinley had been a too-willing compromiser as well as a strong believer in the wisdom of public opinion. And at the time, presidents were not in the habit of using the White House as a "Bully Pulpit" (as his successor Theodore Roosevelt would say) in order to mold popular sentiment. Another path for McKinley could have been to give strong support to powerful members of the Senate, such as Nelson W. Aldrich, William B. Allison, Mark Hanna, Hoar, Orville H. Platt, and John C. Spooner, all of whom had acted earlier to block resolutions recognizing the Cuban rebels or giving them the status of belligerents. The president could have also allied himself with the powerful Speaker of the House, Thomas B. Reed, who was adamantly opposed to a war with Spain. But McKinley failed to take any of these men into his confidence and thereby stiffen the legislators' resolve to stand against war.

Instead, from the time he took office, McKinley's method of avoiding war had been to say as little as possible about the Cuban situation. He said nothing about Cuba in any of his public addresses, and he remained silent when the *Maine* exploded and sank. Not wanting war, yet not wanting to buck public opinion, he became paralyzed to act and allowed himself to slide into a war he dreaded. Later, he confided to a former private secretary, "[The] declaration of war against Spain was an act which has been and always will be the greatest grief of my life. I never wanted to go to war with Spain. Had I been let [alone] I could have prevented [it]. All I wanted was more time."[27] This pronouncement may have been wishful thinking in retrospect, but it does appear to support McKinley's private opposition to what became the Spanish-American War.

As the cries for war mounted, the president had to take drugs in order to sleep, dark circles appeared around his eyes, and he aged noticeably. A friend who went to see McKinley reported the president "broke down and cried like a boy of thirteen."[28] Finally bowing to pressure from legislators, the newspapers, the Republican Party, and public opinion, he asked Congress for a declaration of war "in the name of humanity, in the name of civilization, [and] in behalf of endangered American interests."[29] Congress obliged and declared war on April 25. In the House of Representatives, the vote for war was overwhelming—311 to 6. In the Senate, it was closer at 42 to 35. According to the war resolution, the war would be fought "for the recognition of the independence of the people of Cuba, demanding that the Government of Spain relinquish its authority and Government in the island of Cuba, and to withdraw its land and naval forces from Cuba and Cuban waters, and directing the President of the United States to use the land and naval forces of the United States to carry these resolutions into effect."[30] At the last moment, Spain, bowing to the request of Pope Leo XIII, pledged it would declare a unilateral armistice in Cuba. By then, it was too late; the United States was determined to fight. Besides, Congress, the press, and the public at large were demanding Spain be punished for sinking the *Maine*, even though there was still no proof of Spanish culpability. In addition, most Americans believed a war to liberate Cuba was entirely altruistic—a gesture of morality and kindness toward the Cuban people.

Demands for war were also grounded in the negative views of Spain and of the Spanish people held by most Americans, who had imbibed these prejudices from various sources but especially in school. Textbooks invariably presented the Spanish as greedy and cruel, which allegedly stemmed from the basic Spanish character, and condemned the way Spain had treated the Indians of South and Central America—while conveniently ignoring the cruelty of English settlers toward Native Americans, actions that continued under the government of the United States in the decades after independence. The Spanish, it was also claimed, had no capacity for good government, and Spanish culture was rooted in the superstitions of medieval Catholicism. Such views of Spain and its people made it easy, indeed automatic, for Americans to assume Spanish authorities in Cuba had purposely, with malice aforethought, blown up the *Maine*, even though there was no conclusive evidence, and even though logic and common sense would strongly suggest they had nothing to gain and everything to lose by doing so.[31]

Neither the president nor Congress had stated any specific war aims beyond the liberation of Cuba. McKinley insisted that no nation could set specific war aims in advance and that the course of war would shape the consequences of the conflict. These pronouncements could be interpreted as reflecting modesty on his part, but they may also have indicated national arrogance: Americans liking to think they could deal with anything that might arise. In truth, the outcome of any war is likely to be unpredictable no matter how much nations want to believe otherwise.

Tellingly, neither the president nor Congress as a body said anything about annexing the Philippine Islands or other possessions— or what the consequences of such annexations might be. Before the Spanish-American War began, McKinley had only the vaguest notion of where the Philippines were located. One day, US senator Joseph B. Foraker of Ohio came to see the president to introduce him to a man seeking a consular post in the new administration. The president apologized, saying the only post he had left was in a place called Manila, "somewhere way around on the other side of the world." McKinley added he "did not know exactly where, for he had not had time to look it up." Indeed, as late as December 1897, the president confessed he could not "have told where those darned islands were within two thousand miles."[32] This ignorance is even more remarkable because news of a rebel uprising in the Philippines against their Spanish masters had been reported in the American press for more than a year. Clearly, the president did not regard the islands as significant to American national interests or well-being.

Although the United States was ill prepared for war and made a number of blunders in executing it, Spain, which had been in decline for centuries, was no match for the United States. In about six weeks, American forces were victorious on all fronts. The US Navy smashed Spain's Atlantic and Pacific fleets and defeated Spanish land forces in Cuba, Puerto Rico, and the Philippines.

The question remains whether armed American intervention was necessary to secure Cuban independence. By the time war was declared, some fifty thousand Cuban rebels had occupied most of

the island, and it may have been only a matter of time until they prevailed. Since Theodore Roosevelt was determined to take part in the
invasion, he feared just such an outcome—that the rebels might win
before American troops had landed.[33]

So when the war broke out, Roosevelt resigned as assistant secretary of the navy, against McKinley's wishes, and took charge of a
New York State militia unit that came to be known as the Rough
Riders, which he had been organizing in secret for several months.
Although he was thirty-nine years old, had terrible eyesight, and was
the father of six children whose mother had been seriously ill all
winter, Roosevelt was determined to seize what he figured would be
his last chance to experience war. He told one friend he was going to
fight even if it meant leaving his wife's deathbed. Other friends tried
to talk him out of it. One wrote, "I really think he is going mad. . . .
Roosevelt is wild to fight and hack and hew."[34]

Although Roosevelt was an ardent expansionist, he also had personal goals for going to war. All his life, he had been ashamed that
his father had hired a substitute rather than fight in the Civil War.
It did not matter that his father had done so out of regard for the
sensibilities of his Southern-born wife, whose brothers were fighting
for the Confederacy. Tellingly, Roosevelt maintained a great admiration for his mother's two brothers who had been officers in the
Confederate Navy. It apparently did not bother him that these uncles
had been part of an orchestrated attempt to overthrow the United
States government in the South. What mattered was that they had
been warriors and therefore deserved admiration. In addition,
Roosevelt wanted to test his own manhood. He had been a sickly,
asthmatic child who had built himself up by sheer will. It takes no
deep knowledge of psychology to conclude he continued to harbor
doubts about himself. According to historian John Milton Cooper,
"In a sense [Roosevelt] never fully matured. Throughout his life he
showed an adolescent's incessant need to prove himself."[35]

As a youth, Roosevelt had reveled in tales of mythic warriors from
ancient days. His favorite was Henry Wadsworth Longfellow's epic
poem "The Saga of King Olaf," first published in 1863. From its very
first lines, it proclaims the glories of bravery and sacrifice in battle:

"Strike the sails!" King Olaf said;
"Never shall men of mine take flight;
Never away from battle I fled,
Never away from my foes!
Let God dispose
Of my life in the fight!"[36]

Another lifelong Roosevelt favorite was the *Nibelungenlied* (or *Song of the Nibelungs*). Like "The Saga of King Olaf," the *Nibelungenlied* praises the heroic deeds of intrepid warriors. Its opening lines read:

Full many a wonder is told us in stories old,
of heroes worthy of praise, of hardships dire,
of joy and feasting, of weeping and of wailing;
of the fighting of bold warriors, now ye may hear wonders told.[37]

To Roosevelt, a war with Spain would allow him and his brave countrymen to rejuvenate themselves and their pampered society. War would be an ennobling, spiritual experience, like he and others of his generation wanted to believe the Civil War had been for soldiers on both sides. As Roosevelt had declared in his speech to the Naval War College, peace was all well and good, but too much of it would enervate the national spirit. He took up this theme in his autobiography as well: "I believe most earnestly and sincerely in peace, but as things are yet in this world the nation that cannot fight, the people that have lost the fighting edge, that have lost the virile virtues, occupy a position as dangerous as it is ignoble."[38]

In the spirit of the ancient warrior tales that had long enthralled Roosevelt, he and his officers drank a toast shortly before disembarking for Cuba: "To the officers—may they get killed, wounded, or promoted."[39] Although the Rough Riders, as their name suggests, were a cavalry unit, there was only enough room on the transports for the mounts of the officers. Thus, in the famous charges that Roosevelt led up the hills overlooking Santiago, most of his men had to advance on foot.

Roosevelt first led his men up Kettle Hill and, on taking it, launched a second charge up the parallel San Juan Hill. He seemed under the spell of an uncontrollable inner drive as he pushed himself and his men forward. In trying to describe what he had felt that day, he wrote, "All men who feel any power of joy in battle know what it is like when the wolf rises in the heart."[40] He felt no sorrow about the carnage all around him but, rather, exulted in it: The Rough Riders had lost 89 men, and Roosevelt noted with pride that they had suffered the greatest losses of any American cavalry regiment in the fighting. And surveying the bodies of the enemy, he had exclaimed to a fellow trooper, "Look at all these damned Spanish dead."[41] In fact, Roosevelt had long gloried in killing as a hunter who slaughtered animals with abandon, not for game but for sport. Now, as a warrior, he was thrilled by killing men while risking his own life and the lives of his soldiers in wild charges against the enemy. Some years later, William Howard Taft, Roosevelt's secretary of war and then president himself, had it exactly right when he wrote, "[Theodore] loves war. He thinks it is essential to develop the highest traits of manhood, and he believes in forcible rather than peaceful methods."[42]

Roosevelt the war lover now had had his "crowded hour," a phrase he borrowed from an eighteenth-century poem by Thomas Osbert Mordaunt (which once had been attributed erroneously to Sir Walter Scott):

> Sound, sound the clarion, fill the fife!
> Throughout the sensual world proclaim,
> One crowded hour of glorious life
> Is worth an age without a name.[43]

The poem, with its paean to the glories of heroic battle, echoed the old warrior sagas so dear to Roosevelt. At last, he had expunged the shame over his father's failure to fight. "I am quite content to go now," he wrote to his close friend Henry Cabot Lodge, "and to leave my children at least an honorable name." Being awarded the Congressional Medal of Honor would seal this status, he thought. In case he died prematurely, he asked Lodge to continue to work for the prize to be awarded posthumously. As he put it to Lodge with his usual lack of modesty, "I should awfully like the children to have it, and I think I earned it."[44] Medal or not, he would always cherish his brief adventure in Cuba as "the great day of my life."[45] (In 2001, 103 years after his great day, Congress would finally award Roosevelt the Medal of Honor.)

The vast majority of American soldiers who died in the war over Cuba had not lost their lives as warriors on the battlefield. Although 345 of them perished in combat, 5,462 died of sickness because of lax sanitation practices, tropical diseases, and an almost total lack of sufficient medical facilities and care. Although fortunate himself to escape any sickness during the war, Roosevelt was appalled by the army's failure to meet even basic sanitary and medical needs. Despite being the most junior officer at a military health conference in Cuba, he drafted what was called a "round-robin" letter, which the other members agreed to sign, and gave it to the Associated Press. Neither the War Department nor President McKinley was happy about this criticism, but the order came for the men to move out.

Roosevelt and nearly all the Americans who fought in Cuba were contemptuous of the Cuban rebels they had purportedly come to support. When the Cuban revolt broke out in 1895, Americans had not bothered to distinguish the Cubans from the Spanish and held a dim view of both. To separate the rebels from the negative perceptions of the Spanish, the press, along with various spokespersons for intervention, used a number of methods to distinguish between the two and thereby make the rebels sound deserving of American help. One method was to associate the rebel cause with the American Revolution and the "Spirit of '76." Protestant clergy in the United States, drawing on a long history of anti-Catholicism, claimed the Cuban rebels were being oppressed by the Catholic Church. But the fact that many of the rebels were either black or brown posed a real problem at a time when nearly all Americans, northerners and southerners alike, believed nonwhites were inherently inferior to whites. The solution was to assert, against all evidence, that most of the rebels were white. American opinion makers also downplayed the guerrilla nature of the insurgency, which included terrorism against anyone who did not side with the rebels, as well as the wholesale destruction of enemy property. Instead, the rebels were depicted as fighting in well-organized, conventional units at a time when civilized warfare was defined by how armies were made up.

When American forces arrived in Cuba, they were shocked to see that most of the rebels were not white and that they bore no resemblance to a regular army. Equally appalling to the Americans was the rebels' filthy clothing, torn and full of holes. American commanders quickly decided the rebels were of no use to them as fighters and would be better employed as manual laborers (doing the kind of work most black people were forced to perform back in the United States at the time).[46] Roosevelt had nothing but contempt for the Cubans, calling them "the grasshopper people" who were "nearly useless."[47] One Rough Rider wrote home that all of them were "miserable hounds . . . niggers or half breed[s]."[48] In fact, the rebels had kept the Spanish troops at bay while Roosevelt and the American troops were advancing at Las Guasimas in Cuba. All in all, Americans had gone to war imprisoned by racial and ethnic stereotypes, fueled by incredible ignorance about the Cuban people.

The failure to prepare for sanitary and medical needs was as disgusting as it was unforgivable. Appalling, too, were the racism and ignorance toward Cuba and the Cubans. Yet in the wake of American victory, Secretary of State John Hay could call it "a splendid little war."[49]

The war was indeed "splendid" for Theodore Roosevelt, who, having a great knack for publicity, had taken photographers to Cuba with his unit, along with two very early movie cameras and their operators. His sister Bamie had also cultivated on his behalf the celebrated Richard Harding Davis, a reporter for Hearst's *New York Journal*. Davis's dashing dispatches about Roosevelt helped make him a hero to an adoring American public. After returning home, Roosevelt added to his personal luster by writing a book called *The Rough Riders*, which was serialized in *Scribner's Magazine*. Although Roosevelt was somewhat surprised by the intensity of his fame as a warrior, he had helped to lay the groundwork for it and was more than happy to take advantage of it to get elected governor of New York in 1898 and vice president of the United States two years later. McKinley's assassination in September 1901 would propel him into the presidency, and as president, he would preside over an inglorious war in the Philippines that he had played a large role in launching.

CHAPTER 3

CONQUERING THE PHILIPPINES

"The Philippines form our heel of Achilles. They are all that makes the present situation with Japan *dangerous*."

—Theodore Roosevelt

On May 1, 1898, just eleven days after Congress declared war, Admiral Dewey executed his orders to attack the Spanish fleet in Manila Bay. He easily dispatched the decrepit flotilla, losing only one man. An English historian later described the battle as "a military execution rather than a real contest."[1] Having achieved his immediate objective, Dewey was uncertain what to do next. His only orders had been to destroy the Spanish fleet, but he assumed he should go ahead and take the city of Manila itself. In any case, the American fleet could not stay in Manila Bay indefinitely without resupplying, and all the ports in Asia were closed to Dewey under international law because his nation was officially at war. He could have steamed back to the United States, which would have seemed a repudiation of his victory, and face an outraged public that had exulted over his success. This would have been the best decision in the long run. Instead, realizing a land force would be needed to occupy Manila, Dewey cabled Washington for troops. This request and the subsequent delivery of soldiers led to a wholly needless war of conquest in the Philippines that cost the lives of thousands, including women, children, and old men.

President McKinley now found himself in a quandary over what to do with the Philippines. Taking the islands had never been part of the initial war aims, either in McKinley's reluctant statements about the need to fight Spain or in Congress's declaration of war, which had called only for liberating Cuba. Indeed, the Teller Amendment to the war resolution had explicitly stated the United States would not annex Cuba but would leave "control of the island to its people." According to this formula, the United States would help Cuba to win independence and then withdraw all forces. It would have made abundant sense to apply this same policy to the Philippines, but the president said nothing for weeks following Dewey's smashing victory. Even when Gen. Wesley Merritt set sail for the Philippines in June 1898, along with some twelve thousand troops, McKinley gave him only vague instructions. Merritt was to "reduce Spanish power in that quarter" and establish "order and security to the islands while in the possession of the United States."[2] What the president did not say was how long that possession would last, mainly because he had not decided what to do. Above all, McKinley continued to be a consummate politician who closely followed public opinion and the views of other leading Republicans while revealing very little about his own thoughts. So he waited to see where the wind was blowing before deciding what to do with the Philippines.

Not at all anticipated at the beginning of the war in the Philippines—though it should have been—was a Filipino rebellion against the United States. In August 1896, Filipino rebels had risen against the Spanish authorities who had ruled the islands for more than three hundred years. The rebels were eventually led by Emilio Aguinaldo, a member of a well-to-do family who had served as the mayor of Cavite el Viego, his hometown. In March 1897, the rebels established the Republic of the Philippines, with Aguinaldo as president. At the end of 1897, after the two sides had fought to a standoff, Aguinaldo agreed to a peace with Spanish authorities. The Spanish government in the Philippines, fearing the United States was about to go to war over Cuba, was anxious to end the fighting in the islands. Aguinaldo claimed the government promised reforms in the Philippines that included amnesty for the rebels, Filipino representation in the parliament, and a reigning in of Catholic religious orders that owned or controlled much of the land and levied taxes on the people. (In truth, the Spanish authorities did not intend to carry out these commitments—and did not do so.)

Agreeing to go into exile, Aguinaldo received a large sum of money from Spanish authorities. He claimed to have accepted the money to purchase weapons for renewing the struggle, though a less compelling explanation is that the Spanish simply bought him off.[3] In any case, he went into exile in Hong Kong and then in Singapore, where he met the American consul, E. Spencer Pratt. According to Aguinaldo's diary account of their exchange, Pratt had consulted with Admiral Dewey before their meeting. In Aguinaldo's words,

> Pratt said Dewey replied that the United States would at least recognize the independence of the Philippines under the protection of the US Navy. The consul added that there was no necessity for entering into a formal written agreement because the word of the Commodore and the US consul were in fact equivalent to the most solemn pledge, that their verbal promises and assurances would be honored to the letter. . . . The consul concluded by declaring, "The Government of the United States is a very honest, just and powerful government."[4]

Dewey later denied ever making such statements through Pratt, adding, "In short, my policy was to avoid any entangling alliance with the insurgents, while I appreciated that, pending the arrival of our troops, they might be of service."[5] In any case, Aguinaldo returned to Hong Kong, where he was taken aboard an American cutter and transported to Manila.

Adding weight to Aguinaldo's confidence the Americans were sincere in supporting independence for the Philippines was the cable he sent before leaving Hong Kong. To revolutionaries back home who were continuing to resist Spanish rule, Aguinaldo expressed his joyous belief the United States had come to liberate them:

> Divine Providence is about to place independence within our reach. The Americans, not from mercenary motive, but for the sake of humanity and the lamentations of so many persecuted people have considered it opportune to extend the protecting mantle to

our beloved country. . . . There where you see the American flag
flying, assemble in number; they are our redeemers![6]

In a second, equally optimistic cable, he referred directly to the
American tradition of liberty:

> Filipinos, the great nation, North America, cradle of liberty and
> friendly on that account to the liberty of our people . . . has come
> to manifest a protection . . . which is disinterested towards us, con-
> sidering us with sufficient civilization to govern by ourselves this
> our unhappy land.[7]

Even if Aguinaldo had not received any definite promises of
independence during his discussions with the Americans, it is under-
standable he would think the United States would help the Philippines win independence. His reflections on the American Revolution and his knowledge that the United States had forsworn any idea
of annexing Cuba would have only buttressed his confidence about
the benign intentions of the Americans.

Once back in the Philippines, Aguinaldo again assumed leadership of revolutionary forces. He and his men took control of much
of Cavite Province, located on the southern shores of Manila Bay,
from which they advanced on Manila, in the process taking more
than two thousand Spanish prisoners and surrounding the capital
city. They also captured important towns on Luzon (the largest and
most important of the Philippine Islands, which includes Manila),
along with some smaller islands in the archipelago.

On June 12, Aguinaldo announced the Philippine Declaration
of Independence from Spain. He also set up a capital at Malolos,
a substantial town north of Manila; held the first session of their
legislative body; and made good progress toward establishing civil
government throughout Luzon. The Political Constitution of 1899
gave wide autonomy to the provinces and included a bill of rights
to protect individual liberties. Despite this progress toward a viable
government, General Merritt ordered the Filipino troops to remain
where they were as his troops entered Manila. In August, the Americans accepted the surrender of Spanish forces without consulting

the Philippine Revolutionary authority and put in place an American military government. After having helped significantly to defeat the Spanish forces, the rebels could only regard this as an outrageous act of betrayal.[8] Accordingly, in January 1899, Aguinaldo issued a warning to the Americans:

> My government is ready to open hostilities if the American troops attempt to take forcible possession of such portion of the territory as comes under its jurisdiction. I denounce these acts before the world, in order that the conscience of mankind may pronounce its infallible verdict as to who are the true oppressors of nations and the tormentors of human kind. Upon their heads be all the blood which may be shed.[9]

From the beginning of the American presence in Manila, Aguinaldo asked Merritt to recognize the Philippine Republic and made the same request of Merritt's replacement, Gen. Elwell S. Otis. Both refused. Of course, it was not within these generals' power to grant this request, but they could have urged the administration back in Washington to give it serious consideration. Aguinaldo also sent an envoy named Felipe Agoncillo to the United States to try to negotiate independence for the Philippines. When President McKinley received him on October 1, 1898, Agoncillo expressed his and Aguinaldo's admiration for the American political system and their wish to follow it as a model. He also brought up the meetings Aguinaldo had had with the American consul in Singapore, who allegedly supported Filipino independence. In addition, Agoncillo asked to take part in the forthcoming peace talks in Paris between the United States and Spain. After ignoring claims of American support for independence, McKinley told Agoncillo he could go to Paris—not as an official representative but merely to plead his case to the peace commissioners.[10] Agoncillo arrived in Paris only to have both the American and Spanish commissioners refuse him a hearing.[11]

From Paris, Agoncillo went back to Washington, where he sought to speak with several officials in the McKinley administration, all of whom ignored him. He then composed a memorandum stating the case for Philippine independence and sent it to the State Department. His points were thorough and well reasoned: The Philippine independence movement was influenced by the American example; the revolutionaries had established and maintained a government resembling that of the United States; and since Spain was only in possession of Manila at the time the peace treaty was signed, Spain no longer had any sovereignty over the rest of the islands.

(Those familiar with the origins of the Vietnam War cannot help but see the similarities: When Ho Chi Minh sent letters to President Truman and his administration asking for recognition of Vietnamese independence and pointing out the parallels between Vietnam's quest for independence and the American Revolution, he received no response.[12] Agoncillo was at least received at the White House, though his entreaties were ignored. In both cases—the Philippines in 1898 and Vietnam in the late 1940s—war could have been easily avoided if the president of the United States had acted on requests to recognize the independence of much-oppressed peoples.)

Although McKinley had dispatched American forces to secure Manila, he continued to be silent about how long they would remain there and whether the United States would extend its rule throughout the entire Philippine Islands. Among the options were (1) retaining just a naval base and coaling station for refueling ships, (2) taking over the principal island of Luzon, and (3) annexing the entire archipelago.

As a summary of McKinley's reasons for wanting to annex the Philippines, historians have often quoted remarks he reportedly made to a group from the General Missionary Committee of Methodist Church on November 21, 1899. The president, unable to decide what to do about the islands, had supposedly confessed,

> I walked the floor of the White House night after night until midnight; and I am not ashamed to tell you, gentlemen, that I went down on my knees and prayed Almighty God for light and guidance more than one night. And one night late it came to me this way—I don't know how it was, but it came: (1) That we could not give them back to Spain—that would be cowardly and dishonorable; (2) that we could not turn them over to France or Germany—our commercial rivals in the Orient—that would be bad business and

discreditable; (3) that we could not leave them to themselves—they were unfit for self-government—and they would soon have anarchy and misrule over there worse than Spain's was; and (4) that there was nothing left for us to do but to take them all, and to educate the Filipinos, and uplift and civilize and Christianize them, and by God's grace do the very best we could by them, as our fellow-men for whom Christ also died.[13]

Historians have often mocked these pronouncements as examples of McKinley's ignorance about the Philippines in particular and East Asia in general, along with his claims that God had told him what to do. McKinley biographer Lewis L. Gould doubts these quotations are exactly what McKinley said that day, since they were not reported until more than three years later, when one of the visitors, James F. Rusling, published them as an interview with the president in a religious magazine.[14] McKinley was indeed a devout Christian, and there is no reason to question that he prayed about what to do with the Philippines or that he may indeed have believed his prayers had clarified the issues. But the reasons for annexation that supposedly came to him through a divine message late one night were suspiciously similar to those that various individuals and groups had been advocating ever since Dewey's victory at Manila Bay.

Putting aside speculation about what McKinley believed God had revealed to him, the president's reasons for why the United States should annex the Philippines remain very much open to criticism. One wonders if the president knew 90 percent of Filipinos were Roman Catholics. Of course, given the intense anti-Catholicism in the United States at the time, he may have been thinking Protestant missionaries could go into the islands and save them from their errant beliefs. McKinley could legitimately argue that, given Spain's total defeat, allowing the Spanish to remain in control of the islands was not a reasonable alternative. However, there were indications that the Filipinos, some of whom had taken part in the Spanish administration of the islands, were quite capable of independence and responsible self-governance. Furthermore, independence would mean the United States would not have to consider turning the Philippines over to any commercial rivals. All in all, independence was the least troublesome, least costly, and most rational option, especially if the United States genuinely wished the Filipinos well and aided their independence. But as diplomat and historian George Kennan put it, "The American people of that day . . . simply liked the smell of empire and felt an urge to range themselves among the colonial powers of the time, to see our flag flying on distant tropical isles, to feel the thrill of foreign adventure and authority, to bask in the sunshine of recognition as one of the great imperial powers of the world."[15]

Then there was the desire to increase trade with China, which led to claims an American presence in the Philippines would put the country in a better position to assert its trading rights in the Middle Kingdom. According to the diplomatic historian Richard Leopold, "The desire for the Philippines and a concern for China became mutually supporting."[16] In reality, the Chinese people, most of whom lived in abject poverty at the time, were hardly promising trading partners for American goods, but the facts about Chinese markets meant little to McKinley as he campaigned for Republicans in the congressional elections in the autumn of 1898. In Iowa, he proclaimed, "What we want is new markets, and as trade follows the flag it looks very much as if we [are] going to have new markets."[17]

Later, when speaking in Omaha, Nebraska, the president was less than honest about the origins of the war. The United States had not sought the war with Spain, he insisted. Nor, he claimed, had the nation wanted the new international responsibilities that had come with the war, but now, the American people had to show "the courage of destiny," as if the war and its outcome were somehow preordained as an updated version of manifest destiny.[18]

In Indiana, meanwhile, the young Republican orator Albert J. Beveridge had become one of the most outspoken advocates for annexing the Philippines. In a speech in Indianapolis at the party's September meeting to inaugurate the 1898 fall campaign, he insisted again and again that taking the islands had been ordained by God himself. "Fellow Americans," he cried, "we are God's chosen people. . . . We cannot retreat from any soil where Providence has unfurled our banner." Furthermore, God had ordained the destruction of the Spanish fleet at Manila Bay: "His power directed Dewey in the East and delivered the Spanish fleet into our hands on the eve of Liberty's natal day, as he delivered the elder [Spanish] Armada into the hands of our English sires two [actually three] centuries ago."[19]

Both the defeat of the Spanish Armada and Dewey's triumph at Manila Bay, Beveridge proclaimed, were manifestations of a divinely appointed Anglo-Saxon race: "It is the tide of God's great purpose made manifest in the instincts of our race, whose present phase is our personal profit, but whose far-off end is the redemption of the world and the Christianization of mankind." And in answer to those who said people should not be governed without their consent, Beveridge answered that this concept applied only to "those who are capable of self-government." In case his audience did not get the point, he went on, "We govern the Indians without their consent, we govern our territories without their consent, we govern our children without their consent." The obvious implication was that the Filipinos were like either savages or children (or both) who could not possibly sustain independence and self-rule.[20]

Toward the end of the fall campaign, on October 28, 1898, McKinley cabled the American peace commissioners in Paris that they should demand annexation of the entire Philippine archipelago. The rationale put forward was "right of conquest," but this was a weak claim in international law, since the United States had not yet occupied Manila when Spain sued for peace in July. To overcome this objection, the United States agreed to pay Spain $20 million to help defray the Spanish debt in the islands. In addition to the Philippines, the United States claimed and received Puerto Rico and Guam, the latter an island in the Marianas chain located in the western Pacific. In July, through a joint resolution of the Senate and House of Representatives, the United States had annexed Hawaii to provide coaling stations for its ships, then powered by coal and steam, as well as a forward naval base.

If Aguinaldo and those supporting the Philippine Republic still held out any hope the United States would honor their fervent desire for independence, McKinley's proclamation of December 21, 1898, issued a week and a half after the signing of the peace treaty with Spain, dashed such a notion. "With the signature of the treaty of peace," it declared, "the future control, disposition, and government of the Philippine Islands are ceded to the United States." Further-more, "In the fulfillment of the rights of sovereignty thus acquired . . . the actual occupation and administration of the entire group of the Philippine Islands becomes immediately necessary, and the mili-tary government . . . is to be extended with all possible dispatch to the ceded territory."[21]

Between August 1898 and early February 1899, an uneasy standoff existed between the American occupiers and the Filipino revolution-aries. Then, on February 4, General Otis authorized American troops to advance toward Filipino lines just outside the city. At one spot that night, an American sentry shot and killed three Filipino soldiers, touching off an exchange of fire. In the day-long fighting that fol-lowed, approximately three hundred Filipinos died, while forty-four Americans were killed outright or mortally wounded. Otis later said he did not believe Aguinaldo had actually "wished to open hostilities at that time," a recognition that the Filipinos did not then plan to start an armed conflict with the United States.[22] Otis also reported that Aguinaldo had gone so far as to send one of his associates under a flag of truce, who told the American general the fighting had been contrary to Aguinaldo's orders. In addition, Otis revealed that Agui-naldo offered to establish a neutral zone wide enough to keep the two armies apart and prevent future incidents. But Otis refused, saying the fighting must continue "to the grim end."[23]

Otis's earlier orders for troops to approach Filipino lines just outside the city were clearly provocative. And contrary to what actually happened on February 4, the McKinley administration told newspaper reporters the insurgents had attacked Manila. The yellow press raged in indignation that Filipinos had dared to "fire on the flag." (Sixty-five years later, in August 1964, provocative actions by the US Navy just off the coast of North Vietnam would similarly provide an excuse to open the shooting phase of the United States–Vietnam War).

When McKinley received the news late on the evening of February 5 that hostilities had commenced in the Philippines, he reportedly remarked to an associate, "It is always the unexpected that happens. . . . This means the ratification of the treaty; the people will insist on its ratification."[24] Some historians have believed the outbreak of hostilities convinced three senators who had been against the peace treaty with Spain, which provided for annexation of the Philippines, to change their minds and vote in favor of it.[25] It is difficult to know for sure, since a number of factors determined the outcome of the treaty vote. Of prime importance was the instruction to senators by William Jennings Bryan, the leading Democrat and that party's presumptive candidate for president in 1900, to vote for the treaty so failure to ratify would not hurt his political prospects. And one should not discount the generous distribution of federal jobs to the home states of the opposing senators to secure their support.[26]

An overarching justification for annexing the Philippines, besides the dubious economic arguments and the misguided assertion the Filipino people needed to be Christianized, was the widespread assumption white Europeans and their descendants in the United States (especially those of Anglo-Saxon ancestry) belonged to a superior race. Proclaiming this belief in the same month war broke out in the islands was a poem by British author Rudyard Kipling that appeared in the American *McClure's* magazine. The initial, most often quoted lines read:

> Take up the White Man's burden, Send forth the best ye breed
> Go bind your sons to exile, to serve your captives' need;
> To wait in heavy harness, On fluttered folk and wild—
> Your new-caught, sullen peoples, Half-devil and half-child.[27]

Kipling's was a none too subtle call for Americans to join their British counterparts in imperial ventures for the supposed benefit of humankind. This sense of a shared Anglo-American burden of civilizing the benighted peoples of the world would go far in binding the former mother country and her former colonies in a common cause and helping put an end to decades of animosity and mistrust. But to the American opponents of annexation, seeing their country behave like imperialist Britain was a shameful betrayal of the American Revolution. Equally inconsistent, the United States had officially declared war on Spain to free the Cuban people from their cruel Spanish overlords. Yet somehow, supporting the Filipino bid for independence from Spain was out of the question.

Whatever the arguments for going to war in the Philippines, they did not meet one of the core requirements of a just war: "necessity and last resort." Independence for the Philippines posed no threat to the United States, particularly if coupled with some truly benign agreement of protection. And the war was not a last resort, especially since Aguinaldo and Agoncillo had reached out the hand of friendship to the United States. Nevertheless, President McKinley pressed ahead with orders to put down the "rebellion" in the islands—which was, in fact, a fight for independence against a new colonial master. In any case, the national security and well-being of the United States did not require the conquest of the Philippines. There was no "supreme emergency" the country had to meet with force of arms.

From the beginning of his command in the Philippines, General Otis had underestimated the number of troops he would need to put down the "insurrection," and he sent one rosy report after another back to Washington about the progress he was making with the war and the ease with which the "enemy" would be defeated. In late 1899, he told Secretary of War Elihu Root that the local population regarded the Americans as liberators and the insurgency had been broken. His successor, Gen. Arthur MacArthur (the father of famed World War II general Douglas MacArthur), continued to make overly optimistic pronouncements about how the war was going. Only when an Associated Press article questioning such pronouncements was smuggled out of Manila and published in newspapers back in the United States did the McKinley administration become alarmed about the war.[28]

Making the situation more intractable in the Philippines was the widespread belief of many, if not most, of the Americans stationed there that they were indeed racially superior to the Filipinos. Although it is common in wars to use verbal slurs to define the enemy, such words are not always explicitly racist. During World War II, Americans referred to the Germans as "Krauts," and during the Civil War, Union forces referred to Confederate troops as "rebels," while Southerners used the term "Yankees" (or even "Damned Yankees") for their Northern foes. In the Philippines, however, the dark-skinned people were often called "niggers" by the American troops. In so doing, they were transferring racist attitudes toward African Americans, held at the time by most US residents, to the people of the Philippines.

Historian Paul A. Cramer, in his article about racial attitudes toward the Filipinos, gives numerous examples of this sorry phenomenon: One black American soldier reflecting on his experience in the Philippines believed war would not have broken out "if the army of occupation would have treated the [Filipinos] as people." Instead, they began "to apply home treatment for colored peoples: cursed them as damned niggers, steal [from] them and ravish them, rob them on the street of their small change, take from the fruit vendors whatever suited their fancy, and kick the poor unfortunate if he complained."[29] Racial slurs were frequent in the letters US troops sent back home. One sergeant wrote, "Have I written any of you folks since we commenced to chase niggers [?]"Another trooper wrote they had gone after "a strong hold of the niggers." Yet another commented they were having "lots of sport to hunt these black devils."[30] American journalists reported on the widespread use of the words "nigger" and "niggers" among the US military in the islands. One of them, Henry Loomis Nelson of the *Boston Herald,* remarked, "Our troops in the Philippines . . . look upon all Filipinos as of one race and condition . . . and being dark men, they are therefore 'niggers,' and entitled to all the contempt and harsh treatment administered by white overlords to the most inferior races."[31]

Another slur used for Filipinos was "goo-goo" (also spelled "gugu"). One soldier wrote home about "fights with the 'Guggoes.'" Another wrote, "They were the first goo-goos I ever saw turn white."[32] Although the origin of the term is unclear, some linguists believe "goo-goo" evolved during the early twentieth century into "gook" which was used to refer to any Asian people. Tellingly, the term "gook" would be used extensively to refer to the Communist enemy in the Vietnam War.[33]

Aguinaldo and the Filipino leadership were well aware of how white Americans treated black people in the United States— depriving them of basic human rights and enforcing discrimination through violence and threats of violence, including lynching and savage beatings. That American troops called Filipinos "niggers" only stiffened their resistance to being conquered.

Since the Filipino troops were no match for the firepower of the Americans, Aguinaldo fell back on guerilla tactics as the only way to continue the struggle. The Filipinos did not stand and fight in uniforms as members of standard military units but wore civilian clothes and blended into the countryside, a strategy Aguinaldo adopted in mid-November 1899. And instead of fighting against well-armed Americans in conventional battle lines, they engaged in hit-and-run attacks and ambushes. They hoped such a strategy would wear down the American forces in the islands, as well as public opinion back home, so the invaders would eventually leave.

However, as Aguinaldo feared, the Americans immediately branded them as uncivilized savages, since civilized people were thought to wage conventional wars characterized by fighting in uniforms as members of well-defined units.[34] (The Americans had conveniently forgotten they themselves had sometimes resorted to irregular, hit-and-run tactics against better-armed British troops in the American Revolution, especially in the southern theater of war.)

According to Gen. Arthur MacArthur, who took over command of US forces in the Philippines in January 1900, the guerillas owed their continued success to the "almost complete unity of action of the entire native population."[35] But MacArthur believed that after the presidential election of 1900 resulted in McKinley's reelection, the time would come to take whatever measures were necessary to crush the Filipino rebels. Indeed, the day after the election, McKinley met with his cabinet and forwarded orders to MacArthur to "start a vigorous campaign at once, pressing the remnants of the Filipino army to the last extremity."[36] On December 20, MacArthur proclaimed martial law throughout the Philippines and warned guerilla fighters they would be treated as outlaws. "Men who participate in hostilities without being part of a regularly armed force," he added, must "divest themselves of the character of soldiers and if captured are not entitled to the privileges of prisoners of war."[37] That same month, Gen. James F. Bell sent some 2,500 men on a search and destroy mission. He ordered that "all able-bodied men . . . be killed or captured," adding, "These people need a thrashing to teach them some good common sense."[38] Bell also directed his commanding officers not to tolerate any neutrality on the part of the Filipinos: "Every inhabitant . . . should either be an active friend or classed as an enemy."[39] In addition, anyone suspected of aiding the enemy was to be arrested and held indefinitely, with or without firm evidence. (Those familiar with the indefinite detention of suspected terrorists during the Iraq War or the classification of Vietnamese people as either for or against the United States or its South Vietnamese ally will immediately see the parallels.)

There are many accounts of American troops torturing Filipinos to obtain information from them. A trooper named Clarence Clowe, in a letter to US senator George Frisbie Hoar of Massachusetts, described in chilling detail the methods he and the other men employed: "At any time I am liable to be called upon to go out and bind and gag helpless prisoners, to strike them in the face, to knock them down when so bound, [and] to bear them away from wife and children, at their very door, who are shrieking pitifully. " Clowe added the Americans showed no "repulsion" in using such methods. "On the contrary," he wrote, "the majority of soldiers take a keen delight in them, and rush with joy to the making of this latest development . . . a Roman holiday."[40] Incredibly, many such letters were written to newspapers back home, which published them with all the gruesome details.

The most notorious torture was what American troops called the "water cure" (known also as the "water torture"). In a letter from November 1900, a Sergeant Riley described the ghastly procedure. The victim in this case was a head of a village, whom Riley called "the Presidente." When the man evaded some questions the Americans asked of him, they administered the cure:

> This was done by throwing him on his back beneath a tank of water and running a stream into his mouth, a man kneading his stomach meanwhile to prevent his drowning. The ordeal proved a tongue-loosener, and the crafty old fellow soon begged for mercy and made full confession. . . . The Presidente was asked for more information, and had to take a second dose of "water cure" before he would divulge.[41]

It is thought the Americans learned of the water cure from the Filipinos, who, in turn, had learned it from the Spanish, who had used it to torture victims during the Spanish Inquisition. The Americans used the term "water cure" because they believed it would "cure" its victims of any sympathy with the rebels. Theodore Roosevelt, early in his presidency, wrote in a private letter to German diplomat Speck von Sternberg that the water cure was "an old Filipino method of mild torture. Nobody was seriously damaged whereas the Filipinos had inflicted incredible tortures on our people."[42] In fact, the treatment was hideously painful. Those who had to endure it felt they were being drowned and strangled to death at the same time. And as their internal organs were pressed and convulsed by the tremendous water pressure against them, they felt as if they were being cut to pieces and burned alive.[43] Americans administering this torture even had themselves photographed while doing so, apparently with no fears that these images would be used to incriminate them. (In the Iraq War, the United States would resort to a similar form of torture, by then called "waterboarding.")

The *Philadelphia Ledger*, a pro-administration Republican newspaper, virtually gloated in a November 1901 description of the brutal methods American forces were using against the Filipinos:

> The present war is no bloodless, fake, opera bouffe engagement; our men have been relentless, have killed to exterminate men, women, children, prisoners, and captives, . . . an idea prevailing that the Filipino as such was little better than a dog. . . . Our soldiers have pumped salt water into to men to "make them talk," and have taken prisoners of people who held up their hands and peacefully surrendered, and an hour later, without an atom of evidence to show that they were even insurrectos, stood them on a bridge and shot them down one by one, to drop into the water below and float down, as examples to those who found their bullet-loaded corpses.[44]

The worst atrocities carried out by American forces occurred in September 1901. To retaliate for an attack on an American garrison in Balangiga, a small village in Samar Province, Gen. Jacob H. Smith demanded draconian punishment for the entire province. In an interview he gave to the *Manila Times*, Smith quoted the orders he had given: "I want no prisoners. I wish you to kill and burn: the more you kill and burn, the better you will please me." Furthermore, Smith wanted everyone over ten years old to be killed, since Samar boys were as dangerous as the older men. "Kill and burn," he directed, and "make Samar a howling wilderness."[45]

Smith carried out this campaign by ordering the entire population of Samar into various towns or concentration camps. Their villages were torched and burned to the ground, as surviving photographs by American forces testify. Anyone found outside these zones was to be summarily executed. Thousands died of disease and malnutrition in the detention areas. The camp deaths, added to those executed, resulted in an estimated 8,344 deaths between January and April 1902.[46] (Such tactics had been used by the Spanish in Cuba. The United States denounced them as examples of Spanish cruelty and used them to justify declaring war on Spain. Yet when these methods were used by Americans in the Philippines, they were somehow acceptable to many.)

The atrocities at Samar shocked the public back home. Besides that, the war in the Philippines had been an unanticipated, ugly surprise for most Americans, and it became more and more unpopular as it continued for month after month and year after year. Secretary of War Elihu Root believed one way of quieting the domestic opposition was to recruit native Filipino troops to fight the guerrillas. It would save American lives, possibly shorten the war, and probably save money in the long run. The British had long used native troops throughout their empire to put down rebellions and maintain order, especially in India. Now, American expansionists, who tended to be strong Anglophiles, found this example compelling. And British army officers were not shy about offering advice. One wrote to the *Daily Chronicle* of London, "The Americans have still much to learn. They do not seem to understand the game, which is to use one set of natives against another."[47]

US senator R. F. Pettigrew warned Root that using some Filipinos to fight others risked turning the conflict into a civil war. He also warned that the only native troops likely to enlist as mercenaries under the American flag were the Macabebes, a group who were traditionally hostile to the majority Tagalogs in Luzon. The Macabebes had often fought as mercenaries under Spanish authorities in the Philippines and had been essential for putting down rebellions and keeping the Spanish in power.[48] According to Pettigrew, Root himself had admitted the Macabebes were known to "murder, burn and rob" and were difficult to restrain "within the lines of civilized warfare."[49] The Macabebe Scouts, as they were called, turned out to be fierce and effective fighters and did, in fact, contribute greatly to breaking the rebel resistance. It was also thought that the Macabebes instructed the American troops "in the fiendish expedient of the 'water cure.'"[50]

Well-documented atrocities committed by Americans in the Philippines helped to stoke an anti-imperialist opposition. Some critics of the war in the Philippines joined the Anti-Imperialist League, but others remained independent of any organization. Although the anti-imperialists often disagreed with each other on ideas and tactics, a situation that weakened their message, they shared a core of beliefs. They feared that acquiring an overseas empire would thrust their country into the maelstrom of international politics and intrigue. And by extending the nation's responsibility for far-flung possessions in Asia and the Pacific, the United States made itself liable to intimidation or attack by other powers. It was also obvious to the anti-imperialists that a larger army and navy would require huge financial outlays, resulting in a greater burden to American taxpayers. In addition, they feared that the increased money and attention given to foreign matters would distract from pressing problems at home. Imperialism, they charged further, betrayed the nation's own revolutionary heritage. Having rebelled as colonists against Great Britain, the United States was now playing the role of imperial oppressor. For the anti-imperialists, it was impossible to reconcile the American principles of representative government and the protection of individual liberties with the current American policies of violent conquest and governing colonial subjects without their consent. Sadly, some of those who opposed taking the Philippines did so for racist reasons; this was especially true of southerners, who did not want to risk bringing more people of color into the American family.

The great majority of anti-imperialists considered the war in the Philippines to be grossly immoral, since there could be no excuse for slaughtering and torturing people who only wanted their freedom.

Furthermore, they believed the United States should work to bring about change in the world through example—not through force. Most of all, perhaps, imperialism betrayed the long-held belief in American exceptionalism. Americans wanted to believe their country was a New Eden and a beacon of hope to all humankind. Now the United States was acting like any other world power—and, in the process, trampling on the very values its own citizens supposedly held most dear.[51]

The anti-imperialists included in their ranks some of the best-known and most admired individuals in the United States. These included former presidents Benjamin Harrison and Grover Cleveland, industrialist Andrew Carnegie, union leader Samuel Gompers, Harvard president Charles William Eliot, philosopher William James, reformer Jane Addams, and author Mark Twain. The stronghold of the Anti-Imperial League was in Boston, where many members associated their crusade with the city's earlier leadership in the antislavery movement and its devotion to the Union cause in the Civil War.

In February 1901, Mark Twain wrote a stinging criticism of his country's ongoing war in the Philippines for the prestigious *North American Review*.[52] After the United States had helped Cuba win its independence and then decided to conquer the Philippines, Twain pretended puzzlement at this contradiction. "There must be two Americas," he wrote, "one that sets the captive free, and the one that takes a once-captive's new freedom away from him, and picks a quarrel with him with nothing to found it on; then kills him to get the land." Setting Cuba free Twain called the "American game," and subduing the Philippines he called the "European game," an example of which was then being played out by the British, who were fighting the Boers in South Africa. Had his country instead played the "American game," Twain said, "Dewey would have sailed away from Manila as soon as he had destroyed the Spanish fleet—after putting up a sign on shore guaranteeing foreign property . . . and warning the Powers that interference with the emancipated Filipino patriots would be regarded as an act unfriendly to the United States." Twain charged that in order to conceal this betrayal, President McKinley and the supporters of annexation were playing a double game—talking of bringing freedom and civilization to the Philippines while creating an empire: "We were only playing the American game in public—in private it was the European [game]." Toward the end of his article, Twain unleashed a crescendo of sarcasm:

> There have been lies: yes, but they were told in a good cause. We have been treacherous; but that was only in order that real good might come out of apparent evil. True, we have crushed a deceived and confiding people; we have turned against the weak and the friendless who trusted us; we have stamped out a just and intelligent and well-ordered republic; we have stabbed an ally in the back and slapped the face of a guest; . . . we have invited our clean young men to shoulder a discredited musket and do bandit's work; . . . we have debauched America's honor and blackened her face before the world; but each detail was for the best.

Andrew Carnegie, upon being invited to a reception to honor the commissioners who had negotiated the peace treaty with Spain, wrote a refusal laced with bitter irony: "Unfortunately I shall be in Pittsburgh the evening of your reception to the signers of the War Treaty with Spain, not the Peace. It is a matter of congratulations however that you seem to have about finished your work of civilizing the Filipinos. It is thought that about 8000 of them have been completely civilized and sent to Heaven. I hope you like it."[53]

Another critic was the young poet William Vaughn Moody:

> Lies, lies! It cannot be: The wars we wage are noble,
> And our battles still are won for us, ere we lift the gage.
> We have not sold our loftiest heritage.
> The proud republic hath not stooped
> to cheat
> And scramble in the market-pace of war. . . .
> Ah no!
> We have not fallen so.[54]

In March 1899, a little over a month after the Senate had ratified the treaty with Spain, which included American annexation of the Philippines, two dozen anti-imperialists drew up a manifesto asking President McKinley to proclaim an armistice and convene peace talks in Washington with Filipino representatives. The president and his military advisors dismissed the plea and said there could be no peace negotiations until the rebels agreed to surrender completely to American authorities—that is, give up control of their own land to foreign invaders.

Undeterred, the anti-imperialists pressed on with their criticisms and were denounced as traitors in Republican newspapers for giving "aid and comfort to the enemies of their country." As the presidential election of 1900 approached, they were referred to as "Copperheads" (that is, poisonous snakes), a term used during the Civil War to denounce Peace Democrats in the North. This label was especially inappropriate because so many of the older anti-imperialists had been staunch defenders of the Union. This fact was lost on Union veterans, assembled for their annual encampment of the Grand Army of the Republic the previous summer, who denounced members of the Anti-Imperialist League as unworthy to be called American citizens. They apparently could not see that while they had fought to free a people from bondage, the war in the Philippines was being fought to deny a people their freedom. For them, all wars Americans fought were just, and those who disagreed were traitors. (Six and seven decades later, many World War II veterans would hold similar views of those who opposed the war in Vietnam, even though the two conflicts were very different.)

At the beginning of the 1900 presidential campaign, as reports of American casualties and atrocities against Filipinos continued to filter back home, many leading Democrats believed the Republicans were vulnerable on the Philippines. In addition to opposing imperialism in the Philippines, the Democrats again called for currency reform and the regulation of big business. The Republicans predictably nominated McKinley for a second term, and largely through the urging of Senator Lodge, they nominated Roosevelt as their vice presidential candidate. The Democrats turned a second time to William Jennings Bryan, who had lost to McKinley four years earlier. Even though Bryan had supported ratification of the treaty, he now called for eventual independence for the Philippines, combined with an American protectorate over the islands. At the same time, he denounced the continuing war of conquest in the islands. It was, he insisted, an abuse of American power and a betrayal of the country's own revolutionary heritage. He also warned that conquest of the Philippines set a dangerous precedent that would lead to more wars of empire, with all the attendant costs in blood and treasure and further betrayal of the country's principles. Instead of fighting wars of conquest, Bryan insisted, the United States should lead the world through moral and modest example.

It was Roosevelt rather than McKinley who barnstormed the country, denouncing Bryan and the Democrats. The Democrats' domestic policies, he cried, were Communistic. As to expansion, Roosevelt insisted it would bring increased prosperity to the nation. Roosevelt also charged that Democratic opposition to McKinley's policies, by giving hope to the enemy, was causing the deaths of American soldiers in the Philippines. The Republican platform asserted in the face of mounting evidence to the contrary that "every step of the progress of our troops has been measured by a humanity which has surprised even the misguided insurgents." Furthermore, it was the duty of the government "to put down armed insurrection [in the Philippines] and to confer the blessings of liberty and civilization upon all the rescued peoples."[55] Again and again, spokespersons for the administration claimed and would continue to claim that American forces were fighting for the freedom of the Filipino people when, in fact, they were fighting to deny them independence and self-determination. (Similar claims would be made throughout the Vietnam War.)

The Republicans also tried to find evidence the Democrats had been in secret contact with Aguinaldo and the rebels. Beginning in January 1900, Secretary of War Root sent a series of cables to General Otis in Manila to forward any captured documents that might prove such a connection. He also asked Otis if he had found, among either the rebels or US soldiers, any "pamphlets, speeches, or other documents from the United States against [American] authority [in the Philippines]." There is no evidence Otis ever responded to these inquiries. Then, in July of that year, rumors of unknown origin began to circulate in Manila that the Democrats were considering an alliance with the Filipino revolutionaries and that the rebels were actively raising campaign funds for Bryan. Despite there being no evidence to back up these charges, William Howard Taft, who was now heading up a civilian oversight commission in the islands, passed along this gossip to the McKinley administration.[56]

As the campaign continued, it became clear that Bryan's denunciations of imperialism failed to excite the majority of voters, who, despite the continuing fighting in the Philippines, were proud of the new empire and felt good about a return to prosperity at the turn of the century after years of depression. Most Americans did not want to believe their fighting men had brought dishonor to themselves and their country. The Republicans won the White House handily, with a popular vote of 51.7 percent for McKinley versus 45.5 percent for Bryan. In the Electoral College, the victory was even more lopsided at 292 to 155. The election of 1900 had not turned out to be a referendum on imperialism, as the Democrats had hoped and the Republicans had feared.

With McKinley safely reelected, American forces redoubled their efforts to put down the Filipino resistance. These renewed efforts led to even harsher measures, which, through various channels, became known back in the United States. In response to this evidence, anti-imperialists put together a petition to the US Senate in December 1901 requesting a probe into the conduct of the war in the Philippines. The following month, Sen. George Frisbie Hoar asked for a special committee to conduct such an investigation. Henry Cabot Lodge—the junior senator from Massachusetts, a close friend of Theodore Roosevelt, and a strong imperialist—rejected the idea of a special committee. He insisted the investigation be run by the committee on the Philippines, which he chaired; in that way, he could be in a position to limit the damage done to his party and the Republican administration.

The hearings began on January 10, 1902. Even though Lodge managed to exclude some of the most damning witnesses, what did come out was appalling: the water cure and other forms of torture, the execution of individuals without evidence or hearing, the shooting of Filipinos who surrendered peacefully, the concentration camps, and the thousands of Filipinos who died of disease during confinement in the camps. In answer to a written request from Lodge to Secretary of War Root, the secretary responded that some charges of misconduct had been looked into, but nearly all the allegations were unfounded: "The war in the Philippines has been conducted," he insisted, "by the American army with scrupulous regard for the rules of civilized warfare, with careful . . . consideration for the prisoner and non-combatant, with self-restraint and with humanity never surpassed."[57]

Root was clearly not telling the truth: None other than General of the Army Nelson A. Miles had sent a letter to the secretary protesting the "marked severity" of the war in the Philippines. When Root wrote back denying the charge, Miles cited as evidence a report by Cornelius Gardener, the American governor of the Tayabas province in the Philippines. The report contained graphic descriptions of torture and wholesale destruction of villages and crops. It was clear both General Miles's letter and the Gardener report were in Root's hands at the very time he asserted to Senator Lodge that American forces had acted in the Philippines "with self-restraint and with humanity never surpassed."[58] It is also evident Root had received many other reports of American atrocities in the Philippines, nearly all of them from "friendly sources."[59]

While the hearings continued, Roosevelt, now president as a result of McKinley's assassination, delivered a speech at Arlington National Cemetery on Memorial Day 1902. He admitted Americans had committed some abuses in the Philippines. But he claimed that for every abuse by Americans, "a very cruel and treacherous enemy" had engaged in "a hundred acts of greater atrocity." Here Roosevelt was echoing a standard government line that the Filipinos had committed equal or worse acts, as if these justified any sort of behavior by the Americans whose country was claiming the moral high ground in the Philippines.[60] More important, any shirking of the nation's duty in the Philippines would be to yield to "the counsels of unmanly weakness." American soldiers and civilians in the islands, Roosevelt insisted, were "doing a great work for civilization, a great work for the honor and the interest of this nation, and above all for the welfare of the inhabitants of the Philippine Islands. All honor to them; and shame, thrice shame, to us if we fail to uphold their hands!"[61]

In June, the Senate committee broke off its investigations of abuses in the Philippines and never resumed them. Two months earlier, President Roosevelt, in a conscious effort to claim that the perpetrators of atrocities would be brought to justice, had ordered Gen. Adna R. Chaffee, now the American commander in the Philippines, to investigate and punish those who had ordered or carried out atrocities. Arrested and ordered to stand trial was Maj. Anthony "Tony" Waller, who was accused of murdering eleven Filipino prisoners. Although Waller admitted he had ordered the killings (claiming justifiable reasons), he was acquitted of all charges. Also court-martialed were Gen. Jacob Smith, who had set up the concentration camps at Samar, and Maj. Edwin F. Glenn, who was accused of ordering water cure tortures. Glenn was ordered to pay a fine of $50, and Smith was admonished for his behavior. No other members of the military were charged for carrying out or ordering atrocities in the Philippines. By any measure, Roosevelt did not carry through on his promise to ferret out the guilty and have them punished.

Not long before the Senate committee discontinued its investigation of the conduct of the war, Senator Hoar gave an impassioned speech in which he denounced the American conduct in the Philippines, speaking in the cadence and style of a prophet in the Jewish Bible:

> You have slain uncounted thousands of the people you desire to benefit. You have established reconcentration camps. . . . You make the American flag in the eyes of a numerous people the emblem of sacrilege in Christian churches, and of the burning of human dwellings, and of the horror of water torture. Your practical statesmanship which disdains to take George Washington and Abraham Lincoln or the soldiers of the Revolution or of the Civil War as models, has looked in some cases to Spain for your example. I believe—nay, I know—that in general our officers and soldiers are humane. But in some cases they have carried on your warfare with a mixture of American ingenuity and Castilian cruelty. Your practical statesmanship has succeeded in converting a people who three years ago were ready to kiss the hem of the garment of the American and welcome him as a liberator, who thronged after your men when they landed on those islands with benediction and gratitude, into sullen and irreconcilable enemies.

Hoar was one of the most outspoken anti-imperialists, and though a Republican, he had voted against the treaty with Spain. His goal had been to defeat the treaty and then force amendments that would result in complete independence for Cuba, Puerto Rico, and the Philippines following a short period of protection by the United States. In truth, if the treaty had failed, McKinley would most probably have resubmitted it in its original form, and because of an increased number of newly elected Republican senators, it would have passed easily.[62] However unlikely Hoar's scenario was, it would have been far better than using force to subdue the Philippines. Thousands of lives would have been saved, and the United States would not have had to compromise its oft-proclaimed principles.

A break for the United States came on March 23, 1901, when Macabebe scouts, working for the Americans, infiltrated Aguinaldo's headquarters and captured him. They took him to Manila, where, on April 19, he took an oath of allegiance to the United States and recognized American sovereignty over the Philippines. Some of his commanders continued to fight, but on July 4, 1902, President Roosevelt officially declared the war at an end and gave general amnesty. Fighting would continue, however, for another dozen years in isolated pockets of the country.

The best estimates are that about thirty-four thousand Filipinos were killed directly in the war and as many as two hundred thousand civilians lost their lives as a result of both direct and indirect causes. The war in the Philippines claimed 4,234 American lives, more than the 3,549 who had died in the Cuban phase of the Spanish-American War.[63] None of these deaths on either side needed to occur.

Many years later, George Kennan would place the blame for the bloody aftermath of the Spanish-American War in the Philippines on politicians who did not have the courage to go against their own political advantage and emotional appeal: "Having resorted to war for subjective and emotional reasons, we conducted it in part on the basis of plans which, as far as we know, had never been seriously examined and approved by any competent official body."[64]

It was soon clear the conquest of the Philippines made the United States more likely to go to war with a major world power in the future. Although the Japanese did not protest the American annexation of the Philippines in 1899, it was obvious the islands were vulnerable to attack and conquest in the event of an armed conflict between the United States and Japan. Indeed, the difficulty for the United States of fighting a war in the western Pacific against Japan became evident when the Japanese scored several stunning victories in 1904 and 1905 during what is known as the Russo-Japanese War.

As president, Theodore Roosevelt wanted to maintain a balance of power between Russia and Japan in northeast Asia. To that end, he did not want the war between these two powers to end too quickly; rather, he wanted both sides to be "exhausted" and agree to a peace that would not permit either one to emerge completely victorious. "It is in our interest," he wrote, "that the war between Russia and Japan be prolonged, [so] that both powers be as debilitated as possible." Nor did he want "their boundary clashes [to] be eliminated by the conclusion of a peace."[65] In other words, Roosevelt wished to maintain a balance of power in northeast Asia that would preserve American economic interests in the area. It did not seem to bother Roosevelt that prolonged fighting between Russia and Japan would mean more death, more maiming, more agony, and more grieving. He clearly still believed fighting, being injured, and dying in war were the highest and most noble expressions of manhood. Roosevelt's main contribution to the goal of establishing a balance of power in northeast Asia was brokering a peace agreement in 1905—what came to be known as the Treaty of Portsmouth (New Hampshire).

In the immediate aftermath of the Treaty of Portsmouth, the United States moved to placate Japan in the Taft-Katsura Memorandum of July 1905, which emerged from discussions between US secretary of war William Howard Taft and Japanese prime minister Katsura Taro. In the memorandum, the United States accepted Japanese control of Korea in exchange for Japanese recognition of US interests in the Philippines.

However, threatening to undermine these understandings with Japan was blatant racial discrimination against Japanese Americans in California. An editorial in the *San Francisco Chronicle* asserted that it was "a pressing world-wide issue as to whether the high-standard Caucasian races or the low-standard Oriental races would dominate the world."[66] On May 5, 1905, as Roosevelt was working to broker a peace between Russia and Japan, the board of education in San Francisco decided to segregate Japanese children in the primary grades, despite the fact that Japanese children had a reputation as exemplary students, and require them to attend a school in San Francisco's Chinatown. Two days later, San Franciscans established the Japanese-Korean Exclusion League. The league not only endorsed school segregation but also called for an expansion of the federal Chinese Exclusion Act of 1882 to include Japanese and Koreans in the ban on immigration of Asians.

The board of education's action clearly violated the Japanese-American Treaty of 1894, which had guaranteed Japanese residents in the United States complete personal protection. Back in Japan, there was widespread public fury over this insult to their country, especially in light of Japan's new status in the aftermath of the Russo-Japanese War. Secretary Root wrote in a memorandum composed at Roosevelt's direction that the Japanese were a "proud, sensitive, warlike" people who were so prepared for war they could easily take the Philippines and Hawaii from the United States. He added the United States should avoid being forced into an unjust quarrel with Japan "by the action of a few ignorant . . . men" in California.[67] Tokyo sent a formal complaint, calling the segregation policy "an act of discrimination and odium, which is impossible to overlook."[68] There was talk in Japan of war against the United States, and President Roosevelt warned the American commander in the Philippines to prepare for such a possibility. Roosevelt was able to ease tensions by convincing San Francisco to rescind the school segregation order in exchange for what has come to be called the Gentleman's Agreement. Under this informal 1907 agreement, Japan would disallow further immigration to the United States in exchange for Congress's not passing legislation to exclude Japanese immigrants. In this way, Japan was spared formal humiliation, and Roosevelt succeeded in defusing the situation.

But public and governmental anger in Japan over the school segregation order, combined with the belief Roosevelt had cheated Japan out of an indemnity in his brokering of the Treaty of Portsmouth, left a lasting residue of ill will toward the United States. The following year, the Root-Takahira Agreement, signed in November

1908 and named for Secretary of State Elihu Root and the Japanese ambassador to Washington, Takahira Kogoro, attempted to calm the situation. As part of the agreement, Japan recognized the annexation of Hawaii and the Philippines, while the United States recognized Japan's plans to annex Korea and its dominant position in southern Manchuria, which bordered Korea. As Roosevelt was about to leave the presidency, relations with Japan appeared stable, at least on the surface.

Yet the war scare and the obvious rise of Japanese power caused Roosevelt, who had urged the American conquest of the Philippines a decade earlier, to admit in private that he had been wrong. In a long letter in August 1907 to William Howard Taft, who had served as governor general of the Philippines and was now Roosevelt's secretary of war, he wrote, "The Philippines form our heel of Achilles. They are all that makes the present situation with Japan *dangerous* [emphasis in the original]." Roosevelt added the United States should give the Philippines independence as early as possible, which "would remove a temptation from Japan's way."[69] Of course, Roosevelt made no public admission of his great misjudgment. To do so would sully his reputation and suggest nearly all the misery and death during the conquest of the Philippines had been a great mistake.

Be that as it may, Roosevelt wanted the nation to be prepared to defend the Philippines from an attack by Japan. As a means of doing so, he wanted Congress to authorize the building of one large battleship every year in order to create a navy that could operate effectively in both the Atlantic and Pacific oceans—the so-called two-ocean navy. But neither Congress nor the public was willing to expend the huge sums that would be needed. Nor were they willing to station a large army in the Philippines for its defense. However, Congress did agree to the building of a Panama Canal to facilitate rapid movement of warships from one ocean to the other. Until the canal was finished in 1914, naval authorities estimated it would take ninety days, by steaming around the southern tip of South America, to send a naval expedition from the Atlantic to the Pacific Ocean, during which time Japan could, in the words of Admiral Dewey, "capture the Philippines, Honolulu, and be master of the sea."[70] In any case, Roosevelt knew full well that neither the American public nor the

Congress was willing to "permanently accept the Philippines simply as an unremunerative and indeed expensive duty."[71]

In the end, the United States neither gave the Philippines immediate independence nor took the necessary measures (just as Roosevelt had predicted) for defending the islands from a future Japanese attack. In 1916, Congress, by passing the Jones Act, did provide for eventual independence for the Philippines; and, in 1932, the Hare-Hawes-Cutting Act promised the islands independence after ten years. However, plans to grant total independence to the islands were interrupted by the rise of tensions between the United States and Japan and then by the beginning of the war between the two countries in December 1941. In fact, the Japanese bombed Manila on the same day as their attack on Pearl Harbor, Hawaii. (Because of the International Date Line, it was December 8 in the Philippines and December 7 in Hawaii.) As Theodore Roosevelt had predicted, the Japanese quickly defeated American and Filipino forces, many of whom were taken prisoner and died in brutal POW camps. After fierce and costly fighting, in early 1944, the United States recaptured the islands from the Japanese at great cost of lives.

On July 4, 1946, the United States finally gave the Philippines full independence, nearly fifty years after it had been denied them. Tellingly, the people of the Philippines today do not commemorate July 4, 1946, as their Independence Day. Instead, they celebrate their Declaration of Independence from Spain, which was proclaimed by Emilio Aguinaldo on June 12, 1898.

Less than six months after the United States finally granted independence to the Philippines, President Harry Truman arranged to give France $160 million in military aid, which would be used to help defeat a Vietnamese uprising against French colonial rule. Full of self-congratulation after winning World War II, those in charge of American foreign policy had forgotten the hazards of fighting against a people who were determined to have their independence. The tragic war in the Philippines half a century earlier should have been a cautionary tale.

CHAPTER 4

COLD WAR PRELUDE

"The greatest danger that can befall us in coping with this problem of Soviet communism is that we shall allow ourselves to become like those [with] whom we are coping."

—George Kennan

Just as ignorance, arrogance, fear, and political game playing had kept the American people and their leaders from taking a rational, clear-eyed view of the Philippines at the turn of the twentieth century, a similar lack of realism led the United States into the disastrous Vietnam War six decades later. Contributing greatly to this flight from reality was the ongoing Cold War, which began shortly after World War II and lasted until the fall of the Soviet Empire in the early 1990s. The Communist dictatorships in the Soviet Union and elsewhere were, in fact, both corrupt and murderous, and their economic policies were disastrous. That being said, Americans and their leaders allowed their fear and loathing of these regimes to blind them to the facts in Vietnam as World War II came to an end—and in the years that followed. Nor did the media, largely out of fear, do anything to set the record straight.

The term *Cold War* became familiar to Americans from a 1947 series of articles by the highly respected newspaper columnist Walter Lippmann. Actually, the term had been coined two years earlier by George Orwell, anticipating the major theme of his novel *1984*, which appeared in 1949.[1] Orwell's novel presents a world gripped by a constant state of war and held captive by a dictator known as "Big Brother." In the novel, there is no open warfare between powerful nations. Instead, there are proxy wars and psychological conflicts—combined with a constant war mentality.

The main actors in the actual Cold War were the United States and the Soviet Union, which, fortunately, did not fight each other directly in an increasingly dangerous nuclear age. Rather, they did whatever was possible to bring other countries and factions into their spheres of influence or under their direct control—and to discredit opposing alignments. Although American policy makers and the public alike often described these alignments as representing a clear contest between democracy (the free world) and totalitarianism (the Communist world), the situation was far more complex, especially in the underdeveloped third world.

Most Americans were surprised and bewildered when the Cold War resulted within a few years after the end of World War II, yet they should not have been, since the Cold War emerged out of the requirements for defeating both Imperial Japan and Nazi Germany. In the end, it took the full might of the United States, the British Empire, and Soviet Russia to win the war. In the process, the US government had made great efforts to convince its citizens to accept an alliance with the Communist Soviet Union—by emphasizing supposed similarities between the American and Russian people and by painting a hopeful picture of postwar friendship and cooperation. At the same time, it was evident as the war was coming to an end that the Soviet dictator Joseph Stalin would take full advantage of his military occupation of Eastern Europe, which had occurred in the process of defeating Germany.

Both the United States and the Soviet Union craved security after World War II. Most of all, Stalin wished to stay in power. He also wanted his country to be safe from attack and his Communist ideology to survive and thrive. Since approximately twenty-seven million people in the Soviet Union had died in the war, versus four hundred thousand for the United States—or about seventy times as many—Stalin believed his country deserved the lion's share of victory spoils in Europe. And to protect his nation against any future attack from the west, he was determined to create a wide buffer in Eastern Europe by establishing Communist regimes in the so-called satellite countries. These included Poland, Czechoslovakia, Hungary, Albania,

Romania, and Bulgaria. By agreement as the war was winding down, the Soviets also occupied the eastern part of Germany, which they turned into another dependent Communist state.[2]

At war's end, the United States desired to restore a balance of power in both Europe and Asia and create a system of collective security. It also aimed to restore a global economic system to help prevent future depressions like that of the 1930s, which many agreed had contributed significantly to the rise and support of authoritarianism in both Germany and Japan. Promoting democracy wherever possible was also a goal of the United States, stemming from the belief democracies are less likely to go to war with one another.

The "Big Three" wartime meetings President Roosevelt held with British prime minister Winston Churchill and Soviet leader Joseph Stalin, which attempted to work out postwar agreements, showed there would likely be difficulties and frictions between the United States and Great Britain on the one side and the Soviet Union on the other. Once the Cold War began in earnest, these Big Three meetings were widely misunderstood in retrospect, and. for decades, Republicans in the United States excoriated Roosevelt for supposedly selling out to the Communists—or, worse, being a knowing collaborator in a worldwide Communist conspiracy. These charges were wholly groundless, since Roosevelt was clearly neither a Communist nor a socialist. In fact, he had done everything possible in the 1930s to save American capitalism, and his strong Christian faith and belief in democratic institutions ran counter to most everything Marx, Lenin, or Stalin espoused. Such wild accusations were a foretaste of the partisan vitriol that would be spewed forth during the Cold War and that would keep the American people and their leaders from viewing the situation in Vietnam accurately.

The most controversial of these Big Three meetings took place in February 1945 at Yalta, a Soviet resort on the Black Sea. There, the conferees agreed to divide Germany into three occupation zones (with Britain and the United States later agreeing to share their zones in western Germany with France, thereby establishing a fourth zone). Stalin promised to allow free elections in Poland, but only if they were consistent with Soviet security needs. (Stalin thereafter held that such elections were incompatible with his country's safety, thus ensuring Poland would become a Communist satellite state.) Soviet "boots on the ground" also meant the rest of Eastern Europe would very likely become Communist. The Soviets had approximately 125 divisions of seasoned troops in Eastern Europe at the end of the war, and there was nothing the United States and Great Britain could do to dislodge them unless they wanted to launch World War III immediately after the end of World War II, something the American public would neither have understood nor tolerated. Indeed, as soon as the Germans surrendered in May 1945, US senators and House members received mountains of letters and telegrams from parents, wives, and sweethearts demanding their boys be sent home immediately. Accordingly, by the end of 1946, the United States had less than two full army divisions in Europe.

Gen. George Patton, who would become something of a cult figure after his death in late 1945, had proposed right after the war that the United States should join with the recently defeated Germans and attack the Soviet Union. For these remarks, and for his refusal to remove Nazi administrators under his occupation, he was relieved of his command. But for years thereafter, the Monday morning quarterbacks in taverns and barbershops, on the golf links and in club rooms, raged that the United States should have unleashed Patton against the Soviets. No matter that wider American public opinion would not have tolerated such an invasion; no matter that American troops would have been woefully outnumbered; and no matter that the Soviets would enjoy the benefits of internal lines of supply and communication.

In order to end the war against Japan, at a time before the US atomic bomb had been successfully tested, Roosevelt at Yalta very much wanted a pledge from Stalin that the Soviet Union would enter the war against Japan within three months of the German surrender in Europe. Stalin agreed, and he also left Yalta believing he had been given a free hand in Eastern Europe. He had no objection to Britain keeping its far-flung empire or to America continuing its domination of the entire Western Hemisphere and all its overseas possessions.

A gravely ill Roosevelt died on April 12, 1945, just two months after the Yalta Conference. Guiding American foreign policy during the first years of the Cold War, roughly 1945 through 1952, was Roosevelt's vice president, Harry S. Truman. The new president, who hailed from Independence, Missouri, had served as an artillery officer in France with the Missouri National Guard during World War I and, after the war, had opened a men's clothing store in nearby Kansas City, only to have the business collapse in the steep recession of 1923. It was the failure of this business venture that led Truman to enter politics as a way of securing a job and making a living. Drawing on the support of the men he had commanded in the war, Truman won a spot as county judge (equivalent to a county commissioner in other states). He was elected to the US Senate in 1934 and reelected in 1940. Although he had risen with the blessing of Kansas City's corrupt Pendergast machine, Truman was personally very honest; he came to public attention during World War II by presiding over a Senate committee that investigated wartime waste, fraud, and corruption in defense industries and suppliers. The Democrats tapped Truman for vice president in 1944 as a replacement for Henry Wallace, who had served as vice president during Roosevelt's third term but was thought too liberal for the times.

Although it is impossible to know how the experienced Roosevelt would have managed postwar challenges, Truman was unseasoned in foreign affairs and was the only president in the twentieth century not to have a college education. The one time he had traveled outside the United States was during World War I, and he had not held a position in the Senate that dealt extensively with foreign affairs. During his short tenure as vice president, he had talked to President Roosevelt only twice and was not made privy to the president's plans for a postwar world.

Truman was clearly stunned at becoming president, even though he had known Roosevelt was in bad health. To a reporter for the Associated Press, he said, "I pray to God I can measure up to the task." News reporters heard him exclaim he "felt like the moon and stars and all the planets had fallen on me."[3] Truman later came to be widely admired for his honesty and his feistiness, but the nation might have been better off if Roosevelt had not sought an unprecedented fourth term in 1944. A victory that year for a moderate Republican, whose party was desperate to regain the presidency after twelve years, might have also spared the country the vicious partisan attacks against the

Truman administration—and the pressure for the president to make decisions that were not in the best interests of the country.

During his first weeks in office, Truman decided that it was important to act like a president, and to him that meant a decisive, even combative pose. There would be none of the procrastination that had marked Roosevelt's conduct at times, and, above all, he would get tough with the Soviets. When Soviet foreign minister Vyacheslav Molotov paid a visit to the White House on April 23, Truman delivered a blistering lecture on Soviet failures to observe the Yalta agreement regarding Poland. An astonished Molotov answered that no one had ever talked to him like that. The president snapped back, "Carry out your agreements and you won't get talked to like that."[4]

There was still some hope that matters could be smoothed out with the Soviets, but verbal salvos on both sides in early 1946 signaled this was unlikely. On February 9, Stalin declared in an impassioned speech that war was inevitable so long as capitalism existed. The Soviet people therefore had to face further sacrifices to block capitalist aggression. The speech was probably intended more for the Russian people, but it alarmed the former Western allies in World War II. Winston Churchill, now out of office as prime minister, answered for the West on March 5 in his now-famous speech at Westminster College in Fulton, Missouri. Accompanied by President Truman, who shared the platform with him, Churchill warned, "From Stettin on the Baltic to Trieste on the Adriatic an iron curtain has descended across the [European] continent." Although he was not the first person to use the term "iron curtain," his well-publicized address gave it wide currency. Churchill also insisted in the speech that the Soviets posed a "growing challenge and peril to Christian civilization." Only a "fraternal association of English-speaking peoples," he added, could hold them in check—strengthened by American nuclear weapons. Stalin quickly responded by calling Churchill a warmonger.

Those present in the audience that day at Fulton noticed that Truman seemed to beam at Churchill, suggesting he agreed with everything the former British prime minister said. The speech created such a furor that Truman then tried to distance himself from it by saying he had not read the text beforehand. Critics of the Iron Curtain speech included the widely read and respected newspaper columnist Walter Lippmann. He contended that Churchill's sharp words were really an attempt to get the United States to bolster British interests in Eastern Europe and the Middle East and that they would "surely accentuate the antagonism of Moscow far more than they reinforce . . . a peaceable settlement." Privately, Lippmann wrote that Churchill's presentation was an "almost catastrophic blunder."[5]

About two weeks after the speech, Secretary of State James Byrnes received an analysis from George Kennan, then a scholar attached to the American Embassy in Moscow. His analysis was the so-called "Long Telegram" (which ran to some eight thousand words). In it, Kennan attempted to explain recent Soviet behavior. The Kremlin, he observed, took a "neurotic" view of the international scene, which was actually a continuation of a "traditional and instinctive sense of insecurity," not just a product of Communism. Even victory over the Germans had not changed this fact. Not only would the Soviets cling to their acquisitions in Eastern Europe, but they might also try to obtain military bases in Turkey and Iran. They might even try to undermine American democracy itself. However, Kennan observed the Soviets did not want to "take unnecessary risks" and tended to back down "when strong resistance is encountered at any point." And since he believed the Soviets were "still by far the weaker force," it was important for the Western world to develop as much "cohesion, firmness and vigor" as it could "muster."[6] Only in that way could the United States and its allies hope to contain Soviet expansion. Here was a description of the subsequent "containment policy," which became the centerpiece of American Cold War strategy for the next four decades.

Kennan closed by warning against a hysterical reaction to the Soviet problem. The United States, he said, "may approach calmly and with good heart [the] problem of how to deal with Russia." His country should study the situation with "courage, detachment, objectivity, and . . . determination not to be emotionally provoked or unseated by it." Essential to this approach was educating the American public about the realities of the Soviet challenge: "I am convinced that there would be far less hysterical anti-Sovietism in our country today if [the] realities of this situation were better understood by our people. There is nothing as dangerous or as terrifying as the unknown." Perhaps more important, the American people must be courageous and self-confident about their "own methods and conceptions of human society." And, he warned, "The greatest danger that can befall us in coping with this problem of Soviet communism is that we shall allow ourselves to become like those [with] whom we are coping." This was a chillingly prescient warning, given that so many Americans, and especially those in government, would for decades imitate some of the worst tactics of the enemy in the process of trying to defeat it.

President Truman was among those who read the Long Telegram—later that year it would help form the basis for a comprehensive examination of relations with the Soviet Union—but it was Secretary of the Navy James V. Forrestal who first rang the alarm.[7] He sent copies to hundreds, perhaps thousands, of high officials as required reading. Kennan's message received even wider coverage when he published, anonymously, the same analysis in the July 1947 issue of *Foreign Affairs* magazine.[8]

Walter Lippmann believed Kennan's analysis was wrong on many points as well as dangerous. He spent fourteen installments of his column, Today and Tomorrow, refuting Kennan point by point. First of all, he believed Kennan had exaggerated the role of Communist ideology in accounting for Soviet behavior toward the outside world. He also asserted that Kennan's containment doctrine, which called for opposing the Soviets at every juncture where they exhibited signs of encroachment, would be to create a "strategic monstrosity" that was doomed to failure and could be carried out only by "recruiting, subsidizing and supporting a heterogeneous array of [American] satellites, clients, dependents and puppets."[9] It would risk unending military interventions, and because many of these "allies" would be dictatorial and prone to provoking revolts, the United States would be faced with supporting autocratic and even tyrannical governments and be accused of "appeasement and defeat and the loss of face."[10] Lippmann added that the real contest between the United States and the Soviet Union was not on the far-flung edges of the Soviet Empire but in the heart of Europe. The solution, he proposed, was a reunification of Germany under firm guarantees of neutrality and demilitarization. Russian fears of being attacked by a rearmed Germany might have sounded ridiculous to Americans, but, given the growing hostility between the United States and the Soviet Union, these fears made a great deal of sense. Lippmann published his columns as a book entitled *The Cold War*, which gave wide currency to the term.[11]

In later years, Kennan came to agree with Lippmann. He denied ever recommending the use of armed force in response to Soviet adventures and deprecated any role he might have played in escalating the Cold War. He also claimed he had intended the doctrine of containment to apply only to Europe—not to the entire globe, as the United States all too often interpreted the doctrine as meaning during the Cold War.

Until 1947, American opposition to Soviet actions was largely strategic and geopolitical. There were protests against the impositions of Communist governments in Eastern Europe, and there were numerous denunciations of Communism per se. But it was not until two years after the end of World War II that many Americans began to interpret all Soviet actions as part of a worldwide Communist conspiracy. At the same time, the United States government became a prisoner of its own anti-Communist rhetoric. Once officials had thoroughly alarmed the public about the Communist menace, any overture toward the Soviets or any response to their peace feelers elicited public and partisan attacks. Thus, Truman and his entire administration were frequently and falsely accused of being soft on Communism. In the Kremlin, too, failure to take a harsher line against the capitalists became a political liability, as factions within the Communist hierarchy vied for power in the years after Stalin's death in 1953. In this sense, both sides became prisoners of their own hardline positions and views of the world.

Unfortunately, American policy makers exaggerated Soviet abilities to wage unceasing war against capitalism. It was true Stalin was responsible for the deaths of millions of his own people. It was also true he and his successors had no respect for basic human rights, which were violated with impunity within the Soviet Union and in outside areas under Soviet control. But this did not mean the Soviets were bent on conquering the entire world. Nor was there any chance of a Communist takeover in the United States, some of the most outspoken fearmongers insisted.

Several other beliefs about Communism that arose during the early years of the Cold War also turned out to be greatly exaggerated or even false. One was the theory of monolithic Communism, which held that all Communism was the same, that there were no meaningful nationalistic divisions among or between Communist states, and that all Communists and their governments were slavish puppets of the Kremlin. This doctrine was clearly in error, as demonstrated by the independent behavior of the Communist government under Tito in Yugoslavia and by the increasing friction between the Soviet Union and China following the victory of Mao Zedong's Communist revolution in 1949. Another belief was the so-called domino theory, which claimed Communism spread in a chain reaction, like a row of falling dominoes placed upright and close together.[12]

Then there was the Munich analogy, named for the failed appeasement at Munich, Germany, in 1938, when the British and French agreed Hitler could take the Sudetenland from Czechoslovakia in return for a promise he would make no further territorial demands. Within six months, he gobbled up the rest of that country. While standing up to Hitler would have been preferable to waiting another year to go to war—thus giving Germany more time to arm itself—applying the lessons of Munich to a country like Vietnam made no sense. Vietnam was not an advanced industrial society that had the capacity to conquer vast territories outside its own borders.

The victory of Mao's Communists over Chiang Kai-shek's Nationalist government in October 1949 presented a golden opportunity for those who wanted to heap abuse on the Truman administration. In fact, the United States had done a great deal to assist Chiang and the Nationalists in the years since the end of World War II. The army had transported Chiang and his troops to Manchuria so they could take control from the defeated Japanese. Truman even dispatched one hundred thousand American troops to China and provided logistical support to the Nationalists. But Mao and the Communists won the race for Manchuria, and when the Russians evacuated the area in 1946, Mao inherited a huge cache of Japanese arms and other equipment.

In December 1945, Truman had sent Gen. George Marshall—who had been army chief of staff during World War II and would later become secretary of state and then secretary of defense—on a fact-finding mission to China, as well as commissioning him to try to bring the Nationalists and Communists into some sort of coalition government. Marshall's mission lasted until January 1947, when he left China without success in mending the rift between the two sides. While there, Marshall decided Chiang was his own worst enemy. His rule was corrupt, incompetent, and tyrannical, and he could not attract the support of the Chinese people, who increasingly sided with Mao and the Communists. In the end, Marshall concluded Chiang could not win the Chinese civil war without massive American assistance, including huge numbers of ground troops and massive air strikes. Indeed, he warned Truman the United States would virtually have "to take over the Chinese government" and remain there indefinitely in the face of fierce and continued Communist resistance.

Truman agreed with Marshall's assessment. As he wrote in his *Memoirs*, "It would have been folly . . . to attempt to impose our way of life [on China] by force." He observed further, "In 1945 and 1946, of all years, such thoughts would have been rejected by the American people before they were even expressed. That was the time when congressmen in Washington joined in the call to 'get the boys back home,' and our influence throughout the world, as well as [in] China, waned as the millions of American soldiers were processed through the discharge centers."[13]

American participation in the Chinese civil war would have become an endless quagmire, and Truman knew it. The administration continued to send Chiang small amounts of aid but believed his cause was lost. For his frank observations and advice on China, Marshall would later be savaged by right-wing Republicans, who accused him of "selling out" to Communism.

Following his victory, Mao made overtures to the United States and even invited the US ambassador to China to meet him for formal talks. Truman nearly gave his assent and then changed his mind, supposing, incorrectly, that Mao was firmly under the thumb of Stalin. Still, the State Department discussed the possibility of recognizing Mao's government as soon as conditions warranted. The China experts in the department, especially John S. Service, who advocated recognition, would soon be excoriated by Republicans as traitors. Again and again, Republicans would also accuse Truman of "losing

China," as if China had somehow belonged to the United States and was subject to American permission to change its government.

An earlier potential opportunity to bring about better understanding between Mao and the United States occurred as World War II was coming to an end. Little known even now, seven decades later, was Mao's request, made to American envoys in China at the beginning of 1945, to fly to Washington to approach President Roosevelt directly about future Sino-American relations. Gen. Patrick J. Hurley, Roosevelt's special ambassador to China, who was devoted to Chiang and the Nationalist cause, delayed sending Mao's request to the White House, and when he did so, it was buried toward the end of a long letter. It is unlikely the seriously ill Roosevelt learned of the request, and, even if he did, he may well have not had the time or the stamina to meet with Mao. Still, one can only wonder what would have happened if Roosevelt had learned of the request and spoken personally with Mao—perhaps with the result that the United States and Mao's China might have started out on a more pragmatic footing.[14] If nothing else, such overtures demonstrate there was a time when implacable opposition to Mao's China was not yet set in stone.

But by 1949, when Mao's Communists were finally victorious and the Cold War was well under way, the American public had been led to believe the contest in China was between a democratic government under Chiang Kai-shek and a cruel dictatorship under Mao Zedong. In fact, both Chiang and Mao were dictators with no respect for democratic processes or basic human rights. But the "China lobby"—a loose coalition of individuals; conservative media; and legislators, especially Republicans—would not let up on Truman and members of his administration. Congressmen Robert Hale of Maine and Walter Judd of Minnesota, joined by Senators Bourke B. Hickenlooper of Iowa and Joseph R. McCarthy of Wisconsin, lambasted Truman for betraying China and pursuing policies that favored the Communists. Another leading spokesperson of the China lobby was Henry Luce, the son of Presbyterian missionaries, who had grown up in China and who published the influential *Time* and *Life* magazines, which together were read by up to fifty million people a week. The main goal of the China lobby was the restoration to power of Chiang Kai-shek and the Nationalists. Luce and other publishers who agreed with him held Chiang up as a model of democracy, despite his record of corruption and despotism, and insisted support for him was an essential test of American patriotism and anti-Communism. They labeled anyone who had suggested any kind of dialogue with Mao's government as a traitor. China experts in and out of government were condemned and mercilessly grilled before congressional investigating committees. And anyone who questioned such tactics was liable to be accused of harboring Communist sympathies—at the very least. Furthermore, the lobby accused the Truman administration and its foreign policy advisors of knowingly and purposely selling out China to the Communists. Republican critics gleefully adopted the rhetorical battle cry "Who lost China?"—with the predictable party answer "Truman and the Democrats."[15]

Mainstream media did essentially nothing to correct the distorted views of the China lobby. Newspapers, magazines, radio, film, and television reported on the Cold War in much the same way they had presented World War II—as a grave national emergency for which all Americans must give their support. So overwhelming was the Cold War consensus well into the 1960s that most media outlets accepted without question what government officials and spokespersons were saying about the conflict. Not until the Vietnam War began to go badly did the media start to question American Cold War orthodoxy. And even if there were doubts among individual reporters and news analysts, none wanted to risk being excoriated by the China lobby or their backers in Congress.[16]

The realities on the ground in China were very different from what the scaremongers were putting forth. China was not a great world power at the time of Mao's victory in late 1949. It was underdeveloped industrially, had no capacity to attract significant amounts of capital, did not have a navy capable of invading any of its neighbors, and was not in possession of a credible air force. Despite its large population (then about four hundred million), it could fight only on the fringes of its own country. In addition, China did not have a history during recent times of trying to conquer its neighbors. Besides, anyone knowledgeable about Far Eastern history knew that China and Russia had long been antagonists and that China was not about to accept dictation from Moscow.

Truman reacted to the lobby's criticism by making unwise decisions to prove he was not soft on Communism. He could, instead, have helped his countrymen have confidence in their own nation as an example to other nations. It was almost as if the American public had come to believe Communist assertions that the ideology was destined to triumph around the world, despite its obvious weaknesses—chief among them that Communism went against human nature and kept individuals as well as whole societies from reaching their full potential. Although Communists never tired of predicting capitalism was bound to destroy itself through its own flaws and inconsistencies, it was, in fact, Communism that was destined to fail because of its fraudulence and internal rot. But in the hysteria over Communism, many Americans did not have sufficient faith that their traditions of freedom and democracy would triumph in the end.

However, given the polarized atmosphere and the political opposition's willingness to pummel Truman no matter what he said, trying to educate the American people would have been extremely difficult for the president. A case in point was the *China White Paper* the State Department released in August 1949. It was actually a large volume of documents and commentary that sought to explain why the United States was not responsible for the defeat of Chiang and the Nationalists. But the publication backfired when Republicans charged that the *White Paper* proved the administration had, in fact, betrayed Chiang and had therefore lost China.

Also problematic for Truman and the Democrats was the timing of Mao's victory. In August 1949, just two months before Mao won the civil war, the Soviets exploded their first atomic bomb, depriving the United States of its nuclear monopoly. From then on, both powers would have to live in fear of a nuclear holocaust, made even more fearful a few years later by the appearance of hydrogen bombs in the arsenals of both sides. Partly in response, Truman ordered his National Security Council to reevaluate the nation's policies toward the Soviet Union and its Communist allies. Their final report, known as NSC-68, would provide a blueprint for the nation's foreign policy for the next three decades.

NSC-68 was largely the work of Dean Acheson, who replaced Marshall as secretary of state in January 1949. The document asserted, without any hard evidence, that the Soviets were bent on dominating the entire Eurasian land mass. Negotiating with them would be futile. They were fanatical Communists who could never be trusted and who would not be satisfied until they had conquered most of the globe. Under the circumstances, the United States had to rebuild its military, stockpiling nuclear weapons and increasing its conventional forces. Additional alliances with non-Communist countries would supplement American rearmament. Finally, the United States should launch an all-out drive to alert citizens of the dangers of international Communism. At the same time, the country should try to undermine the allegiance of the Soviet people to their Communist masters. Communism had to be contained at all costs and perhaps overthrown in the Soviet Union itself.

The overall campaign would require massive appropriations, but there was little chance Congress would make them. Then, in June 1950, Communist North Koreans invaded South Korea, and the money began to flow. The resultant Korean War also meant that there was no possibility the United States would recognize Mao's China any time soon.

The Korean conflict had roots in the aftermath of World War II. Following its defeat, Japan was required to evacuate Korea, which it had formally annexed in 1910. As World War II was ending, the State Department began to think about what should happen to Korea, fearing it might fall into the wrong hands. President Roosevelt had proposed a four-power postwar trusteeship for Korea under the auspices of the United States, the Soviet Union, Great Britain, and Nationalist China. But Roosevelt had died, leaving Truman in charge. Whether such a trusteeship would have worked is uncertain. Historian Bruce Cummings, whose writings on Korea are widely respected, has written that the trusteeship idea, as it evolved, "might have worked to keep Korea in one piece."[17]

Long Telegram author George Kennan doubted such a trusteeship would have been acceptable to the Korean people and, especially, to the Communists in the north. Instead, he thought some sort of neutralization of the Korean peninsula, with both the United States and the Soviet Union agreeing to withdraw their troops at an early period, would have allowed the Koreans to sort out the situation themselves. And if the Communists were to prevail, he believed a Communist Korea might go its own way, not unlike Tito's Yugoslavia, which succeeded in defying Moscow and charting its own course to a large degree.[18] Kennan also recalled in his memoirs that a neutralization of Japan in exchange for a neutralization of Korea, as proposed by none other than General MacArthur, should at least have been tried and might have been successful.[19]

The Soviets' declaration of war against Japan in the late summer of 1945 had entitled them to occupy the northern part of Korea, while American troops took up positions in the south. The 38th parallel, as a dividing line between the two occupying forces, was proposed by State Department officials in Washington as Japan was about to surrender. Stalin accepted the arrangement, though there was no official agreement in writing.

In September 1945, the US Army occupied southern Korea and established a full-fledged military government that remained in place for three years. Within a week of occupying Seoul, American military intelligence identified several hundred conservative Koreans to take up leadership positions. Virtually all of them had collaborated with the Japanese and belonged to the old land-owning elite or wealthy business interests. Because these conservatives were so tainted, the American occupation forces looked for a conservative Korean who had been in exile to serve as a patriotic leader. The US Office of Strategic Services found Syngman Rhee. Despite the objections of the State Department, Rhee was flown into Seoul in mid-October 1945, where he presided over a provisional government and then became president of the Republic of Korea, more commonly referred to as South Korea, when the American occupation ended in May 1948. He held a PhD from Princeton University and had been living in the United States for most of the past thirty-five years.

In the northern part of Korea, leadership was assumed by Kim Il-sung. Kim was a member of the Communist Party who had fought the Japanese in adjoining Manchuria and arrived home in 1945 as a war hero. He was not appointed by the Soviets to head what became the Democratic People's Republic of Korea, known unofficially as North Korea. Rather, he came to occupy that position through his own efforts, which were, in turn, recognized by the Soviet army of occupation. This situation remained after both the United States and the Soviet Union withdrew their occupation forces in 1948.

Both Kim and Rhee were determined to unify the two halves of Korea under their own authority. The United States was fully aware of Rhee's plans and, for that reason, repeatedly refused his request for heavy weaponry, such as tanks and planes, which he could use to attack the north. Stalin also refused to supply Kim with similar weapons so he could invade the south. But following the Chinese revolution in 1949, Kim began to play the Soviets and Chinese against each other, and in early 1950, Stalin reluctantly agreed to supply him with the heavy military equipment he wanted.

Neither Kim nor Stalin believed the United States would take military action to oppose the invasion. One reason for this assumption was a speech Secretary of State Dean Acheson made before the National Press Club in Washington on January 12, 1950. In it, he excluded Korea from America's "defensive perimeter" in Asia. Acheson was, in fact, echoing the consistent position of the Joint Chiefs of Staff, the National Security Council, and Truman himself. It remains uncertain whether Acheson made his statement about Korea purposely or inadvertently, but both Kim and Stalin were quick to pick up on it. Both leaders had miscalculated badly.

Truman was at his home in Missouri on June 24, 1950, when he heard North Korea had invaded South Korea. Although Korea was not then important to the American economy and had been declared just six months before to be outside the country's defensive perimeter, Truman treated the invasion as open aggression across an internationally recognized boundary into a country with an American-sponsored government. Invoking memories of the appeasement at Munich only twelve years before, Truman declared the United States had to stand up to the aggressors. The president wrote, "I remembered how each time that the democracies failed to act, it had encouraged the aggressors to keep going ahead. Communism was acting in Korea just as Hitler, Mussolini, and the Japanese had acted ten, fifteen and twenty years earlier. . . . If this was allowed to go unchallenged it would mean a third world war, just as similar incidents had brought on a second world war."[20] Throughout the Korean conflict, Truman and others in the administration would often invoke the Munich analogy.

In response to the North Korean invasion, Truman quickly sent five American army divisions to South Korea. He also ordered the US Seventh Fleet into the Formosa Strait, a move long demanded by the China lobby in the United States, in case Mao tried to invade Taiwan (formerly known as Formosa). This action meant the United States would, for the next three decades, have to pretend the island of Taiwan, not the massive Chinese mainland, was the real China. It also caused Mao to fear the United States was plotting to use Taiwan as a base for invading China in the future (an action the China lobby strongly advocated).

Truman made these decisions without asking Congress for a declaration of war, instead citing authorization by the UN Security Council to use force against the North Korean attackers. Fortunately for Truman, the Soviet ambassador to the United Nations had walked out of the body in protest against a refusal to seat Communist China as a member of the organization. Truman also insisted the United States was not fighting a war in Korea but "a police action . . . to suppress a bandit raid." In so doing, Truman deprived himself of official congressional support and established a dangerous precedent. Heretofore, American presidents had always sought and received a declaration of war from Congress, as specifically required by the Constitution. With this precedent in hand, future presidents could and would take the country to war, citing their authority as commander in chief of the armed forces, with few effective checks.

Officially, the United States fought in Korea under the banner of the United Nations, with small numbers of troops from other member states, but 90 percent of the armed forces in Korea were American. At first, the war went very badly for the Americans. By the end of the summer of 1950, they were pinned down behind a defensive perimeter around the southeastern port city of Pusan, and it looked as if they might have to evacuate Korea in an ignominious defeat. Then, on September 15, Gen. Douglas MacArthur, commander of US operations, launched a large amphibious invasion at Inchon on the west coast of Korea, not far from Seoul, catching the North Koreans in a pincer movement. The North Koreans now fled back north, crossing the 38th parallel as they retreated. At this point, Truman had achieved his goal of turning back the aggressors.

Having been blasted mercilessly by his critics for losing China and supposedly being soft on Communism, Truman could not resist pursuing the North Koreans all the way to the Yalu River, their border with China, thereby reuniting the peninsula under South Korean president Syngman Rhee. The goal no longer was containing Communism but rolling it back. By late November, American and allied forces were nearly at the Yalu. Truman and his advisors, along with General MacArthur, had dismissed the possibility that China would enter the war, despite a message by diplomatic back channels through India that they intended to do so if the Americans pressed the fighting to the Chinese frontier. On November 25, some three hundred thousand Chinese troops came pouring over the border, and it was now the Americans who were in desperate retreat.

At the time, this Chinese entrance into the war was interpreted by the United States as just another example of the monolithic conspiracy to spread Communism as widely as possible. In fact, Mao had not been informed specifically in advance of North Korea's plan to attack South Korea. Chinese documents released decades later reveal he decided to enter the war only after the United States determined to push beyond the 38th parallel and unite all Korea under the Rhee government in Seoul. Mao did so with great reluctance, worrying his actions might escalate into a full-scale war with a nuclear-armed United States. At the same time, he feared that the defeat of North Korea would allow the United States to station military assets directly along the border with China. The Truman administration had no intention of invading China, but Mao could not know that, especially in light of continuing demands by the China lobby for the United States to assist Chiang in invading the mainland and resuming power there.[21] And because China and the United States had no official relations at the time, there was no way for either side to try direct diplomacy to defuse the situation.

Ratcheting up the stakes was Truman's pronouncement during a news conference on November 30, 1950, that the United States might use atomic weapons to stop the Chinese. He later thought better of what he had said, and he redefined his goal as stabilizing the front at the 38th parallel and achieving some sort of armistice. He reassured his European allies he was not going to use these ultimate weapons or widen the war, but the threat, even though retracted, could not have reassured the Chinese.[22]

General MacArthur, who ironically had earlier proposed neutrality for the Korean peninsula, did not agree with Truman's restraint. For him, North Korea had started the war and should be punished. So, too, should the Chinese feel the sting of massive retribution. MacArthur wanted to blockade the Chinese coast, drop atomic bombs on China, and deploy some thirty-three thousand of Chiang Kai-shek's troops from Taiwan. On March 23, 1951, MacArthur took it upon himself, without Truman's permission, to issue an ultimatum to China. They must agree to conclude an armistice with him in the field or be blown to bits—which further confirmed Mao's worst fears about American intentions toward his country.

MacArthur also appealed over the president's head to Congress. Representative Joseph Martin gave voice to MacArthur's proposal to have Chiang's troops attack the Chinese mainland. And if the United States had not gone to war in Korea to win, Martin charged, then the "administration should be indicted for the murder of thousands of American boys."[23] Henry Luce, as publisher of *Time* magazine and a long-time leading voice in the China lobby, also called for a Nationalist invasion of China.

At that point, Truman decided he had had enough, and on April 11, 1951, he relieved MacArthur of his command for insubordination to the commander in chief. The president knew his action would touch off a firestorm. MacArthur had led American troops to victory over Japan and then presided over the occupation. For many Americans, he was a military genius and illustrious patriot; more than a few voices called for Truman to be driven from office.[24] On the floor of the Senate, Joseph McCarthy shouted, "The son of a bitch should be impeached." Sen. Robert Taft also called for impeachment, albeit more politely. The conservative *Chicago Tribune*, which had never supported the president, declared, "President Truman must be impeached. . . . He is unfit morally and mentally, for his high office." Many other conservative newspapers described the firing as a national catastrophe. Truman was burned in effigy in San Gabriel, California, and baseball fans booed the president when he threw out the first ball at the beginning of the season, long a presidential tradition.[25]

When MacArthur returned to the United States, he received a hero's welcome. There was a ticker tape parade in New York and an invitation to address a joint session of Congress. In his address, MacArthur showed he believed very much in monolithic Communism: "You cannot appease and otherwise surrender to Communism in Asia," he declared, "without simultaneously undermining our efforts to halt its advance in Europe." It went without saying that it was Truman who had surrendered to the enemy. In a final peroration, MacArthur told his rapt audience, "Old soldiers never die, they just fade away—an old soldier who tried to do his duty as God gave him the light to see that duty."[26]

The war in Korea settled into a bloody stalemate in which thousands more Americans died. The American public was not used to their military fighting in such a way. Stalemate was, of course, how the War of 1812 had ended, but that was a long time before and unknown to most Americans at the time of the Korean War. What the public did remember was the unconditional surrender terms that had been demanded of both Germany and Japan, along with the fact that Americans were used to being totally victorious in war. So how, the public wondered, could a nation that had won World War II not manage to defeat a small country like North Korea? Something must be wrong at home: traitors and Communists, it was alleged, had infiltrated the government and kept the country from fighting with all it had.

Various legislative committees began to look into supposed Communist subversion in the federal government. These included the House Un-American Activities Committee, the Senate Internal Security Subcommittee, and the Senate Permanent Committee on Investigations. This last committee became sensationally associated with Republican senator Joseph R. McCarthy of Wisconsin, who chaired it in 1953 and 1954. The committee found no one who had actually betrayed US security or had engaged in disloyal activities, but its accusations were often enough to ruin a person's reputation and career.

McCarthy's activities as an outspoken investigator of allegations of Communist subversion in government began as a result of the speech he made to the Women's Republican Club of Wheeling, West Virginia, on February 9, 1950. In it, he charged, "The State Department is infested with Communists. I have here in my hand a list of

205—a list of names that were made known to the Secretary of State as being members of the Communist Party and who nevertheless are still working and shaping policy in the State Department."[27] Over time, McCarthy kept changing the number of names on this list, which he refused to make public, and no Communists were discovered in the State Department.

Just a month after this speech, McCarthy began going after China experts in the State Department, often known as the "China Hands." His first target was John S. Service, who had spent several years during World War II in China, where he headed the US Observation Group in Yan'an. Because he had written in dispatches that he thought Chiang and the Nationalists were likely to be defeated by Mao's forces, he was accused of being one of the culprits who had lost China. McCarthy also went after two other China Hands, John Carter Vincent and John Paton Davies Jr., both of whom had also reported on what they saw as the dismal prospects of the Chinese Nationalists. Although their careers were ruined, none of the China Hands were ever found guilty of either disloyalty or improper behavior.[28] Unfortunately, their dismissals from the State Department deprived the government of its best experts on China at the very time when such expertise was most needed. And the clear implication was that such traitors in the State Department—not the Chinese people themselves—had led to the victory of Communism in China. Since Democratic administrations had been in power during World War II and the years thereafter, Republicans used these and other charges to bolster their accusations that the Democrats were guilty of losing China. Large segments of the public believed and would continue to believe this charge, even though the US Senate voted 65–22 on December 2, 1954, to condemn McCarthy for "conduct that tends to bring the senate in dishonor and disrepute."[29]

Nevertheless, this atmosphere of fear and unfounded partisan attacks so poisoned thinking about foreign policy, both inside and outside the government, that it became difficult, if not impossible, to rationally assess what was in the country's best interests. It was amid these distortions that the United States became embroiled in the disastrous and unnecessary Vietnam War.

CHAPTER 5

THE VIETNAM DECEPTION

"It is very hard today, to recapture the innocence and confidence with which we approached Vietnam in the early days of the Kennedy administration. We knew very little about the region. We lacked experience dealing with crises."

—Robert S. McNamara

Well before Joseph McCarthy began his attacks, President Truman made a series of fateful decisions that would lead to an American military debacle in Vietnam. At first glance, the similarities between Korea and Vietnam seem evident. Both were divided roughly down the middle, with a Communist regime in control of the northern part and an anti-Communist government in the southern part. Like Kim Il-sung, the leader of North Korea, Vietnamese leader Ho Chi Minh had fought the Japanese during World War II and emerged as a national hero at war's end. However, unlike Vietnam, both North and South Korea developed separate governments that were able to hold the allegiance of their people. Tellingly, South Vietnam was never able to stand on its own without extensive American economic and military support and never developed a true national sovereignty.

Although a Marxist, Ho Chi Minh was familiar with the American Revolution and the principles it represented. He believed the United States, having revolted against the British Empire more than a century and a half before, would be sympathetic to Vietnam's struggle to throw off French rule. But this was not the picture Truman shared with the American people. This discrepancy was the first piece in a massive lie about Vietnam that would last for nearly four decades and end in disastrous defeat for the United States. Not only would five presidents mislead the public about the war in Vietnam, but they would also deceive themselves to greater or lesser degrees. In consequence, the Vietnam War was neither necessary nor a last resort but, in many ways, a grand deception.

Unknown or irrelevant to the vast majority of Americans, Vietnam's independence was proclaimed on September 2, 1945, the day Japan formally surrendered to the United States. After suffering under Japanese imperialism for five years, Ho Chi Minh had no intention of submitting to the French if they tried to reclaim their former Indo-Chinese colonies. The French had governed all or part of Vietnam oppressively during eight decades of colonial rule and left the Vietnamese people worse off than before. In proclaiming his country's independence, Ho quoted from the American Declaration of Independence: "All men are created equal, that they are endowed by their Creator with certain unalienable rights, that among these are Life, Liberty and the pursuit of Happiness." Soon thereafter at a gala celebration in Hanoi, he referred to the recently drafted charter of the United Nations, which called for national self-determination—a principle of the Declaration of Independence that both Woodrow Wilson and Franklin Roosevelt later had embraced as centerpieces of their international polities. Ho even had a band play "The Star-Spangled Banner." He clearly hoped for American recognition, believing the other great powers would follow suit. At the gala, he added if the French attempted to return, the Vietnamese people would "fight to the bitter end."[1] And on that "Independence Day," Ho invited to dinner two members of the American Office of Strategic Services, the precursor of the Central Intelligence Agency (CIA), and expressed his thanks to them for their country's support during World War II, adding he looked forward to a "fraternal collaboration" with the United States in the future.[2]

Ho also wrote several letters to Truman, hoping to open a dialogue with the president. Neither Truman nor anyone in his administration answered these missives; they assumed they could not trust Ho or any other Communist leader. For the third time in about fifty years, the United States failed to respond positively to outreach for support by leaders it would end up fighting. In 1899, McKinley had received Aguinaldo's personal emissary from the Philippines but paid no heed to his entreaties for American support for independence; in 1945, Mao's request for a meeting with Roosevelt had not even gotten to the president's attention; and now, just after World War II, Truman and members of his administration ignored friendly approaches from Ho Chi Minh.

Instead of opening a conversation with Ho, Truman supported France's return to its Vietnamese colony, thereby abetting the worst sort of colonialism in Southeast Asia. The president had come to believe he needed France's support in blocking the spread of Communism in Europe, and he wanted to escape criticism for not holding the line against Communism. Thus, in late 1946 and then in 1947, Truman began sending military aid to the French, including a $160 million line of credit for military aid, knowing it would be used against the rebels in Vietnam.[3] And he did so even though the French themselves believed they faced an uphill battle to reconquer the country. But after being humiliated by Germany in World War II, which included four years of German occupation, France was determined to reassert itself as a great power and thought reclaiming this status required regaining its colonies. But instead of asserting the sort of raw imperial claims that would have been acceptable in another age, France used the cover of crusading against Communism.

In 1947, George Marshall, now secretary of state, reported in a cable to the American ambassador in Paris that the French were unlikely to win in Vietnam. In September 1948, the US State Department itself observed France was "fighting a desperate and apparently losing struggle in Indochina."[4] However, in 1949, the Soviets' first atomic bomb explosion, combined with the Communist victory in China that same year, led Truman, who was reeling from attacks by the China lobby, to send military supplies directly to the French in Vietnam. Then came the North Korean attack on South Korea in June 1950, which opened Truman to more vicious political attacks if he did not continue to support the French, even though he was not optimistic about French success. It was fear of partisan criticism as much as strategic reality that guided Truman on Vietnam.

Of course, there were the obligatory references to the Munich analogy and assertions about monolithic Communism. It did not matter that Vietnam was not Germany, that fervent Vietnamese nationalism would keep Ho from being a lackey to either China or the Soviet Union, or that Communism would not inevitably spill over into Indonesia, the Philippines, Japan, and who knew where else. Besides, as journalist and historian Marvin Kalb has written, "Truman did not have to take this step [in Vietnam]. He could have chosen to fight the Republicans at home and support the French in Europe but not in Vietnam."[5] Instead, Truman prepared the ground for an ongoing American commitment to Vietnam that would end in disaster for the United States two decades later. In fact, his commitment to stop Communism in Vietnam did not still his critics, who continued to flay him for being soft on Communism. In the end, his efforts to deflect criticism by supporting the French in Vietnam did him no good.

Like the costly and unnecessary war in the Philippines at the turn of the twentieth century, the Vietnam War resulted from a toxic brew of ignorance, arrogance, fear, and political posturing. Truman and the four presidents who came after him, who committed the United States to ongoing war in Vietnam, were largely ignorant of Vietnamese history and culture. They held or purported to hold exaggerated fears, which they constantly communicated to the American public, of what would happen if all Vietnam fell to Communism. This fear spilled over into American domestic politics and led presidents to make decisions in the best interests of their parties or reelection prospects—not the best interests of the American people. At the same time, presidents and their advisors asserted that they would have little trouble putting down a Vietnamese drive for independence. Thus, although neither the Chinese nor the Japanese nor the French, had succeeded in subduing the Vietnamese during a total of one thousand years of occupation, American leaders boldly asserted to the public that they could prevail where others had failed.

Dwight Eisenhower, who became president in January 1953, inherited Truman's policy of financial support for the French in Vietnam. When it became clear the following year the French were going to be defeated in Vietnam at the Battle of Dien Bien Phu, Eisenhower privately expressed his disgust for the way they had allowed the enemy to occupy the high ground and then to defeat them. Understandably, he did not intend to send American troops to bail out the French. Just after the war in Korea, he had no desire to get his country involved in another land war in Asia. Nor did he have any patience for the chairman of his Joint Chiefs of Staff, Admiral Arthur Radford, who advocated using nuclear weapons against the Vietnamese Communists. At the same time, Eisenhower wanted to avoid being attacked by conservative Republicans for "losing Vietnam," in the same way they had excoriated Truman for "losing China." So, at a meeting with reporters on April 7, 1954, as French defeat in Vietnam seemed more and more likely, he described what came to be known as the domino theory: "You have a row of dominoes set up, you knock over the first one, and what will happen to the last one is the certainty that it will go over very quickly."[6] The phrase caught on, and soon the domino theory was applied widely to reinforce the doctrine of containment as it supposedly applied to Vietnam.

Yet given Eisenhower's great prestige and popularity, he, much more easily than Truman, could have gotten away with honestly explaining to the American people why any commitment in Vietnam would be a foolish mistake. Although some of the extremists in Congress might have accused him of selling out to the Communists, the vast majority of the American people would not have believed them. Unfortunately, Eisenhower did not adopt this approach.

In 1954, a peace conference in Geneva, Switzerland, took place to deal with the aftermath of French defeat in Vietnam. The end result was the so-called Geneva Accords. The participants agreed to divide Vietnam "temporarily" along the 17th parallel, with the Communists in charge of the northern part and a non-Communist regime in charge of the southern part. Article 6 of the accords made clear this division was provisional "and could in no way be interpreted as constituting a political or territorial boundary." Popular elections in July 1956 would take place throughout the entire country, undertaken by an international commission, which would allow the people of Vietnam to decide what kind of government they wanted in a united country.[7]

The United States sent an observer to Geneva but did not sign the accords. Still, the United States pledged to respect the agreements on Vietnam and do nothing to interfere with their implementation.

Within a year, however, the United States broke its word when it became apparent even the freest elections in Vietnam would deliver an overwhelming victory to Ho Chi Minh and the Communists in both North and South Vietnam. As a result, Eisenhower backed the South Vietnamese government in its refusal to hold elections in the part of Vietnam under its control, a strong indication South Vietnam could not claim to be a separate national sovereignty. Eisenhower also approved additional military aid for South Vietnam and sent military advisors to help build and guide a South Vietnamese army. By the time he left office, the United States had about 1,700 such advisors in the country.

Meanwhile, Eisenhower spearheaded a new alliance system in Southeast Asia. It was superficially similar, as a regional defense system, to the North Atlantic Treaty Organization (NATO), which had been established in 1949 to contain Communism in Europe. This new alliance, the Southeast Asian Treaty Organization (SEATO), aimed to halt the spread of Communism on the opposite side of the globe. By early September 1954, eight nations had signed on. In addition to the United States, the signatories were Britain, France, Australia, New Zealand, Thailand, the Philippines, and Pakistan. Pledging to defend the region, they specifically extended promises of protection to Laos, Cambodia, and South Vietnam. However, the SEATO alliance was significantly different from NATO: there was no joint military command structure, and the alliance was purposely vague, since the member states had different interests. The document also gave parties to the treaty an escape clause by stating that each signatory could limit responses "in accordance with its constitutional processes."[8]

John F. Kennedy, who succeeded Eisenhower, was definitely a cold warrior. While running for office against Republican Richard Nixon in 1960, he accused the outgoing Eisenhower administration of allowing a dangerous missile gap, charging (falsely) that the Soviet Union had many more nuclear-tipped missiles than the United States. Kennedy also accused the Eisenhower administration of having "lost Cuba" to Communism, much in the same way Republicans had accused the Truman administration of having "lost China."

Kennedy's standard campaign speech also asserted, without

actually mentioning Eisenhower by name, that his predecessor had allowed the United States to slip in world standing.

"I ask you to join with me in a journey into the 1960s," he said with great vigor, "whereby we will mould our strength and become first again." Then he added, "Not first *if.* Not first *but.* Nor first *when.* But first *period.* I want them to wonder not what [Soviet Premier] Khrushchev is doing. I want them to wonder what we are doing. I want them to wonder what the United States is doing."[9]

Such speeches did not seem to help Kennedy appreciably, since he continued to lag behind Nixon in the polls as the autumn campaign began in earnest. What allegedly turned the tide was a series of televised debates, a first in presidential campaigning. Throughout the debates, Kennedy more than held his own against Nixon, thereby dispelling the vice president's contention that his challenger lacked judgment and maturity. Kennedy also came across as much more attractive and likable. In the end, Kennedy won by a razor-sharp margin of 113,000 popular votes—not nearly enough for him to claim an electoral mandate.

Unfazed by his narrow victory, at least in public, Kennedy delivered a Cold War peroration upon taking the oath of office that the more cautious Eisenhower would never have given:

> Let every nation know, whether it wishes us well or ill, that we shall pay any price, bear any burden, meet any hardship, support any friend, oppose any foe to assure the success of liberty. This much we pledge and more.[10]

The inaugural speech clearly reiterated Kennedy's stance as a cold warrior. And although he did not specifically say so in the address, the new president subscribed to all the Cold War assertions about Communism, including the domino theory, the Munich analogy, and a belief in monolithic Communism.

Despite Kennedy's lack of a clear mandate, the new president and his administration were bursting with energy and enthusiasm. Historian and advisor Arthur Schlesinger Jr. later wrote: "Euphoria reigned; we thought for a moment that the world was plastic and the future unlimited."[11] Kennedy's secretary of defense, Robert S.

McNamara, reflected many years later on how this atmosphere had contributed to the administration's failure to deal adequately with the situation in Vietnam: "It is very hard today, to recapture the innocence and confidence with which we approached Vietnam in the early days of the Kennedy administration. We knew very little about the region. We lacked experience dealing with crises." And when discussing Vietnam in particular, McNamara lamented, they had failed to ask the most basic questions:

> Was it true that the fall of South Vietnam would trigger the fall of all Southeast Asia? Would that constitute a grave threat to the West's security? What kind of war—conventional or guerilla— might develop? Could we win it with U.S. troops fighting alongside the South Vietnamese? Should we not know the answers to all these questions before deciding whether to commit troops? It seems beyond understanding, incredible, that we did not force ourselves to confront such issues head on.[12]

One reason McNamara and the others did not confront and carefully analyze the issues in Vietnam was their almost-total ignorance of the country. As McNamara later admitted, he himself was nowhere "close to [being] an East Asian expert." He had never been to Indochina, nor did he "appreciate its history, language, culture or values." The same was true, he wrote, "to varying degrees, about President Kennedy, Secretary of State Dean Rusk, National Security Advisor McGeorge Bundy, military advisor Maxwell Taylor, and many others. When it came to Vietnam, we found ourselves setting policy for a region that was terra incognita." McNamara added they also "badly misread China's objectives and mistook its bellicose rhetoric to imply a drive for regional hegemony." Furthermore, they failed to understand "the nationalist aspect of Ho Chi Minh's movement. We saw him first as a Communist and only second as a Vietnamese nationalist," when the truth was exactly the opposite. McNamara also confessed, "Our government lacked experts for us to consult to compensate for our ignorance."[13]

That the government of the wealthiest and most powerful country in the world at the time did not have the necessary experts to help shape a rational Vietnam policy seems incredible. The result was that the nation's top leaders were groping in the dark over Vietnam and would stumble, through ignorance, into one of the greatest foreign policy disasters in American history. The belief they could nevertheless prevail in Vietnam betrayed an equally dangerous arrogance. Besides these factors, Kennedy and his team had an exaggerated fear of Chinese intentions (at a time when there were still no diplomatic relations with China), and they did not want to give Republicans any ammunition for saying they were not doing their utmost to stand up to Communism. (In this sense, the Kennedy White House was not unlike the McKinley administration at the turn of the twentieth century, which had allowed ignorance, arrogance, unreasoning fear, and partisan attacks to lead the country into a wholly unnecessary war in the Philippines.)

If this were not bad enough, the fact finders Kennedy sent to Vietnam consistently brought back conflicting observations and advice. It seems clear, then, that President Kennedy and his administration did not have a good understanding of the situation and were not willing or able to invest the time and energy to shape a realistic policy toward Vietnam—to the detriment of all the people on both sides of the civil war in that country who would be injured, killed, and tormented in the years ahead, as well as the detriment of Americans' faith in their government and the reputation of their country in the world.

It was not Vietnam but Laos that confronted Kennedy as his first crisis in Southeast Asia. Just before Kennedy took office, President Eisenhower told him Laos, which had also been part of the French Empire in Indochina, was in danger of a Communist takeover. Kennedy's new secretary of state, Dean Rusk, agreed with Eisenhower. For years, Rusk had claimed World War II could have been avoided if Britain and France had stood up to Hitler at Munich. Although he admitted Communists in Southeast Asia were by no means equal to the Nazis in the late 1930s, he believed the Munich analogy applied anyway: if Communist aggression were not halted and thrown back in places like Laos, he argued, it would only keep going like the row of falling dominoes President Eisenhower had described.[14]

Ironically, as a young senator, Kennedy had thought the French should clear out of Indochina, that its peoples should be free to chart their own course, and that the United States should not inter-fere militarily.[15] Now, as president, he was being urged by some of his advisors—mainly National Security Advisor Walter Rostow and Gen. Maxwell Taylor, chairman of the president's Joint Chiefs of Staff—to intervene militarily in Laos against the Communist Pathet Lao. But Kennedy thought this was not a sound idea for a number of reasons, including uncertainty over how the Soviets would react. In addition, Gen. Charles de Gaulle, president of France and a man who knew something about the futility of fighting an insurgency in Southeast Asia, advised Kennedy not to send troops to Laos. What Kennedy did decide to do was broker an agreement with the Soviets, the Chinese, and other interested parties, including Britain and France, for neu-trality in Laos. According to the agreement, pounded out at a confer-ence in Geneva from May 1961 to July 1962, a coalition government would be assembled in Laos, and foreign troops as well as foreign military bases would be forbidden in the country. Kennedy and most everyone else in high circles realized such a coalition government would sooner or later lead to a Communist victory, but the arrange-ment had the virtue of buying time and giving the president a good excuse for not sending in troops. In fact, both the United States and the Soviet Union were soon violating the agreement by sending arms and supplies into Laos, but neither side objected, and, in theory, the agreement held.

Neutrality might have been a solution for Vietnam, but Kennedy worried that if he did not take a stand somewhere in Indochina, he would be accused of weakness on Communism. Yet he did not want to commit combat forces and even solicited the advice of retired general Douglas MacArthur, who said it "would be foolish to fight on the Asian continent and . . . the future of Southeast Asia should be determined at the diplomatic table." Seemingly more sober minded than he had been a decade before about committing to an all-out war in Asia, the general added that "there was no end to Asiatic man-power." Even if the United States "poured a million American infantry soldiers into that continent," MacArthur believed, "we would still find ourselves outnumbered on every side."[16] This prediction would be tragically borne out by events. In any case, Kennedy fell back to sending more military advisors to help the South Vietnamese stand up to the enemy and giving millions of dollars of aid to the Saigon regime, but he did not send combat units.

In addition to all the other problems in Vietnam, the conflict in that country was a genuine civil war. It was not just a case of aggression by the North Vietnamese, known as the Viet Minh (an abbreviation meaning the Vietnamese Federation of Independence), against South Vietnam. Rather, it included internecine fighting in the South between Communist supporters, who called themselves the National Liberation Front (NLF) but whose opponents labeled them the Viet Cong (short for Vietnamese Communists), and the non-Communist government in Saigon. Furthermore, the South Vietnamese government, headed by President Ngo Dinh Diem, was corrupt and dictatorial.

In particular, the devout Catholic Diem's murderous repression of Buddhists made it very difficult to paint him as someone who shared American views of democracy and human rights. When Buddhist monks protested peacefully against this repression, they were gunned down by Diem's police. In the end, hundreds were beaten or killed by the regime. Diem's brother, Ngo Dinh Nhu, who was in charge of security, falsely claimed the Buddhist demonstrations were Communist inspired. When monks engaged in self-immolation by having themselves doused with gasoline and set on fire Diem's sister-in-law, Madame Nhu, was heard to say, "Let them burn, and we shall clap our hands."[17] At the same time, Diem's forces were none too effective in fighting Communist insurgents but continued to ask for more American aid. Because Diem was becoming more and more of an embarrassment to the United States, Kennedy gave American operatives in Vietnam permission to help engineer a coup against him. The action took place on November 2, 1963, and, after being captured, Diem was killed. Removing Diem did little good, however, since one coup after another followed, resulting in a lack of direction in the Saigon government. Three weeks later, Kennedy himself was gunned down in Dallas, Texas.

Kennedy had gone to Dallas to try to mend fences with southern Democrats who were angry over his belated support for civil rights. Kennedy had deemphasized civil rights because he feared supporting them could hurt him with southern voters in his 1964 reelection bid.

His Vietnam policies were also being driven in part by reelection strategy, since Republicans were criticizing him for being indecisive on Vietnam and thereby soft on Communism. His aide and personal confidant, Kenneth O'Donnell, reported Kennedy as saying he had made up his mind to withdraw all American forces from Vietnam if he were reelected. Accordingly, O'Donnell said the president had told him, "In 1965 [after the election], I'll be damned everywhere as a Communist appeaser, but I don't care." If he attempted to get out before the election: "We would have another Joe McCarthy red scare on our hands, but I can do it after I'm reelected. So we had better be damned sure that I *am* reelected."[18] Historians have debated over the years whether or not Kennedy would have ended the American commitment to Vietnam after winning a second term. The doubters have contended that Kennedy never would have allowed such a defeat on his watch. which would have handed the Republicans ammunition to use against him and the Democratic Party.

Many years later, Kennedy's secretary of defense, Robert McNamara, reported the president believed winning the war was, in the last analysis, the responsibility of the South Vietnamese. In his memoirs, McNamara quoted an interview Kennedy gave to CBS News anchor Walter Cronkite on September 9, 1963: "I don't think that unless a greater effort is made by the [South Vietnamese] Government to win popular support that the war can be won out there. . . . They are the ones who have to win it or lose it." The United States could give them equipment and send advisors, yet Kennedy added, "I don't agree with those who say we should withdraw. That would be a great mistake."[19] Thus, in the last months of his life, Kennedy seemed to be relying on a kind of dualistic wishful thinking with no real backup plan: He insisted that winning the war depended on the South Vietnamese and that no amount of assistance from the United States would change that. At the same time, he did not think the United States should withdraw, but he did not say what he would do if the South Vietnamese failed to win the war.

It was now up to President Lyndon Johnson, who succeeded the slain Kennedy, to manage the increasingly troubled and increasingly elusive Vietnam situation. Although Johnson was a brilliant (and sometime ruthless) domestic politician, he was not well schooled in foreign affairs and knew next to nothing about Southeast Asia. However, he did worry sincerely about the Communist threat, and he fully accepted the domino theory, the Munich analogy, and a belief in monolithic communism. He was also painfully aware of how Democrats under Truman had been accused of losing China. On November 24, 1963, just two days after Kennedy was assassinated, Johnson told the American ambassador to South Vietnam, "I am not going to lose Vietnam. I am not going to be the president who saw Southeast Asia go the way China went."[20] Looking back after his presidency in a wide-ranging interview with historian Doris Kearns [Goodwin], Johnson explained that his position had been a bit more complicated:

> I knew from the start that I was bound to be crucified either way I moved. If I left the woman I really loved—the Great Society—in order to get involved with that bitch of a war on the other side of the world, then I would lose everything at home. All my programs. All my hopes to feed the hungry and shelter the homeless. All my dreams to provide education and medical care to the browns and the blacks and the lame and the poor. But if I left that war and let the Communists take over South Vietnam, then I would be seen as a coward and my nation would be seen as an appeaser and we would both find it impossible to accomplish anything for anybody anywhere on the entire globe.[21]

Upon becoming president, Johnson did not want to escalate the war until after the 1964 election, when he would run for a full term in his own right. At the same time, he had to show himself tough on Communism during a campaign in which he faced Sen. Barry Goldwater, the Republican nominee. Goldwater called for a stronger stand against Communism and charged that Johnson was not up to the task. Johnson and his team countered by charging that Goldwater was a trigger-happy extremist who well might get into a nuclear war with the Soviet Union. In order to drive home this scare tactic, Johnson's campaign made a television advertisement that has come to be known as "Daisy Girl." The ad opens with a little girl standing in a meadow. Birds are chirping as she plucks the petals from a daisy, counting each one as she goes. When she gets to nine, an ominous voice is heard making the countdown to a nuclear missile launch. With the countdown completed, the screen fills with images of a fiery, all-consuming nuclear explosion. In a voiceover from Johnson, viewers are told, "These are the stakes! To make a world in which all of God's children can live, or to go into the dark. We must either love each other, or we must die." A second voiceover ends the piece, saying, "Vote for President Johnson on November 3. The stakes are too high for you to stay home."[22] In addition, repeatedly during the campaign, Johnson vowed, "We are not about to send American boys nine or ten thousand miles to do what Asian boys ought to be doing for themselves."[23]

Both Johnson and Goldwater exploited Cold War fears for political advantage. Goldwater accused Johnson of not being tough enough on the Communists, while Johnson attempted to frighten the public into believing a President Goldwater would be a dangerous threat to peace. Yet while accusing Goldwater of being a warmonger, Johnson knew full well he would soon have to ratchet up the American involvement in Vietnam. And he managed to do so in a way that could not be held against him, even as the election campaign was getting into full swing. Providing Johnson cover were two reported attacks on America naval destroyers operating in the Gulf of Tonkin in North Vietnam. The first occurred on the night of August 2, 1964, when North Vietnamese Patrol Torpedo boats began firing at the USS *Maddox*. The American ship was not harmed, and no American sailors were killed, while US aircraft in the vicinity sunk one of the Vietnamese boats. Two days later, another US destroyer, the *Turner Joy*, reported during a tropical storm that it was picking up odd radar signals and was probably about to be attacked. The skipper was taking no chances and opened fire.

It is now clear that Johnson and his White House advisors knew there was no attack on that second night.[24] A year later, Johnson commented privately to his press secretary, Bill Moyers, "For all I know, our Navy was shooting at whales out there."[25] Nevertheless, the president went on television that night to tell the American people that there had been hostile actions against the United States in the Gulf of Tonkin and that he had ordered US military forces to take retaliatory action. He also asked Congress for a resolution giving him authority to combat Communist aggression in Vietnam. On August

6, Secretary of Defense McNamara testified before a joint meeting of the Senate Foreign Relations and Armed Services Committees. He reported less than truthfully that the *Maddox* had only been "carrying out a routine mission of the type we carry out all over the world at all times."[26] When asked pointedly, he denied the United States had very recently, on the nights of July 30 and July 31, played any part in South Vietnamese patrol boat raids on the offshore islands of Hon Me and Hon Nieu. In truth, these raids had been carried out by US-trained South Vietnamese commandos under the control of an American special operations unit.

On August 10, both the House and Senate passed the so-called Gulf of Tonkin Resolution by overwhelming majorities. The resolution gave authority to the administration "to take all necessary measures to repel an armed attack against the United States and to prevent further aggression."[27] The resolution did not specify that these measures were valid for Vietnam alone, and so one might argue they applied anywhere in the world. Johnson could have asked Congress for a specific declaration of war against North Vietnam, but, as he explained later, he feared such a declaration might touch off war with China or the Soviet Union, since he did not know if either of these countries had mutual defense treaties with North Vietnam that would require them to defend their ally in a war with the United States.

In fact, the Johnson administration had already come up with the wording of the Gulf of Tonkin Resolution about six weeks earlier, just in case some provocation gave them the opportunity to place it before Congress.[28] In any case, Secretary of Defense McNamara later wrote that Congress never intended the resolution to give Johnson "broad authority to support the escalation that followed. . . . Congress never intended it to be used as a basis for such action, and still less did the country see it so."[29] However, there is no evidence that McNamara argued with Johnson at the time about Congress's more limited intentions.

In any case, Congress had not been told the whole truth about what had happened in the Gulf of Tonkin, but members did not insist on holding their own investigations into what had happened there. Nor did the news media question the administration's line. In many ways, the administration's claims before Congress were reminiscent of the assertions President McKinley had made in early 1899, when he declared that Filipino revolutionaries had started a fight with American troops in the Manila suburbs. In neither instance had the other side chosen to start a war with the United States; in both cases, the US forces had provocatively approached "enemy" lines or enemy territory and then labeled the others as aggressors.

With the Gulf of Tonkin Resolution in his pocket and his reelection to the presidency accomplished in November, Johnson unabashedly did what he accused Goldwater of wanting to do: he began escalating the war. By early 1965, the South Vietnamese army was on the verge of collapse, forcing Johnson to face the prospect of something he had publicly vowed not to undertake—to send "American boys" to do what "Asian boys" in South Vietnam were failing to do. The president began increasing American troop strength in Vietnam and authorizing troops to move from only providing base security and military advice to carrying out combat missions against Communist forces in the South. Over the next three years, Johnson sent more and more troops to Vietnam, until there were more than five hundred thousand fighting there. Not all the president's advisors believed sending combat troops to Vietnam was a good idea. One of them was Clark Clifford, chairman of the president's National Foreign Intelligence Board. Clifford insisted to Johnson in July 1965, "I don't believe we can win in South Vietnam. . . . If we send in 100,000 more men, the North Vietnamese will meet us. If the North Vietnamese run out of men, the Chinese will send in volunteers. . . . I can't see anything but catastrophe for my country."[30]

In February 1965, Johnson also ordered the bombing of supply lines and various industrial and military installations in North Vietnam, even though several of his advisors asserted that the bombing was unlikely to win the war for the United States. Over the next three years, in what was code named Operation Rolling Thunder, the United States dropped more tons of bombs on Vietnam than it dropped in the Asia-Pacific Theater in all of World War II.[31] As some had predicted, the bombing did not bring the North Vietnamese to their knees. On the contrary, according to CIA director Richard Helms in an August 1967 report to Johnson, "Hanoi continues to meet its own needs and to support its aggression in South Vietnam. Essential military and economic traffic continues to move."[32] While the bombing did not stop supplies going south to the Viet Cong, it did kill thousands of civilians and fed the antiwar movement back home.

Throughout the rest of his administration, Johnson received conflicting advice about the war—especially about the successes and failures of the American effort and the prospects for an American victory. And once young Americans were coming home in body bags, Johnson could not and would not consider backing out, for that could be interpreted to mean those who died in Vietnam had died in vain and his presidency was a failure. In public, of course, and especially in televised addresses and news conferences, the president insisted the United States was winning the war, and he often compared Ho Chi Minh to Hitler and the North Vietnamese to Nazis. However, belying these claims was a finally aroused news media reporting from the front, including photographs and film of combat operations.

Until 1963, the news media had not generally questioned the American Cold War consensus and the country's commitment to containing Communism in Vietnam. Nor did they question the despotism of South Vietnamese president Diem, instead emphasizing his staunch anti-Communism. Challenging that view was the rout of South Vietnamese forces, known officially as the Army of the Republic of Vietnam, at the Battle of Ap Bac in January 1963. Many in the American media saw this defeat as evidence the Saigon government was seriously deficient as a military force. Despite assistance from American advisors before and during the battle, the South Vietnamese forces failed to take advantage of their superiority in weapons and favorable battlefield positions. Yet while American reporters emphasized the military shortcomings of the South Vietnamese, they did not question their country's mission to stop the Communists from taking over all Vietnam.

President Diem's murderous persecution of Buddhists in May of the same year likewise resulted in media criticism of South Vietnamese leadership but, again, not the American mission on the peninsula. Over the next few years, the coverage remained generally positive about the overall goal of holding back Communism in Vietnam, even after the United States became directly involved in combat, since virtually all forms of media—newspapers, magazines, radio, and television—reported the war through the lens of a Cold War struggle between the forces of good and evil. By 1967, however, as the war went on without an end in sight, reporters, editorial writers, and broadcast commentators began to question whether the Americans and their South Vietnamese allies were bound to prevail in the end.[33] But because the media still did not question the overall American commitment to Vietnam, there was no attempt by the government to censor what was being reported or said.

The overwhelmingly positive coverage of the Vietnam War during the first years of the conflict was both similar to and different from how media had dealt with the Spanish-American War and the war in the Philippines. The print media, which were all that existed during the earlier conflicts, had acted irresponsibly by pushing the United States into war against Spain and then by being overly supportive during the first months of the American occupation of the Philippines. In the process, they failed to accurately inform the public. However, once American forces started fighting Filipino revolutionaries, and once the extent of American atrocities became known, the press became divided, with many newspapers that were aligned with the Democratic Party expressing criticism of the war. In the case of Vietnam, in contrast (and largely because of the strong Cold War consensus), the media asked few questions about the American mission until the Lunar New Year—the "Tet Offensive" of January 1968. From then until the end of the war in 1975, media coverage was increasingly critical of both the war and the mission underlying it.

During Tet, the North Vietnamese National Liberation Front (or Viet Cong) attacked more than one hundred cities and villages and entered Saigon itself, where they briefly occupied the grounds of the US embassy. American forces beat them back, and, in the end, the offensive failed. Yet the fact the "enemy" was able to pull off these attacks gave the lie to the Johnson administration's claims that the United States was winning the war and that final victory was in sight. In late 1966, for example, Johnson had said to reporters that the United States had enjoyed "an unbroken series of successes."[34] Secretary of Defense McNamara backed him up by claiming, "Military progress in the last twelve months has exceeded our expectations."[35] Both statements were untrue.

Even in the best of circumstances, the administration would have had a difficult time measuring success in a war where there were no battle fronts—unlike World War II, when the leadership and the public alike could draw lines or put pushpins on maps to show progress or retreat. To remedy this problem, the Johnson administration took to using statistics that invariably showed American forces killing more of the enemy than the enemy had killed of them. In 1965, the administration claimed the ratio was 2.2 to 1; in 1966, 3.3 to 1; and in 1967, 3.9 to 1. However, according to numbers supplied to the news media, the ratios were often claimed as closer to 8 or 10 to 1.[36] But as Clark Clifford had predicted, the enemy continued to absorb whatever losses they sustained and fought on. It was also well-nigh impossible to defeat Viet Cong irregular forces (that is, guerrillas) who could hit and run at will and avoid direct contact with the well-equipped "regular" armies of the United States. Such warfare had worked for the Vietnamese for a thousand years against the Chinese, the Japanese, the French, and anyone else who tried to deprive them of independence. For Ho Chi Minh, then, winning the war was a matter of waiting until public opinion in the United States turned increasingly against the war and the Americans were forced by their own people to go home.

Johnson's public addresses in support of the war revealed how determined he was to stay the course in Vietnam and how he disparaged anyone who disagreed with him. In a speech at Johns Hopkins University on April 7, 1965, just a day after he authorized American forces in Vietnam to go on the offensive, Johnson made the argument for war. Although he did not use the term "falling dominoes," he charged that "the contest in Vietnam [was] part of a wider pattern of aggressive purpose" directed by Communist China, which would not rest "until all the nations of Asia [were] swallowed up." The Munich analogy was also there, though again not by name: "Let no one think for a moment that retreat from Vietnam would bring an end to the conflict. The battle would be renewed in one country and then another. The central lesson of our time is that the appetite of aggression is never satisfied."

By invoking this lesson, Johnson was indirectly comparing the Vietnam conflict to World War II. But it was a false comparison.

Although Americans had been reluctant to get involved in World War II, they remained convinced throughout the war that victory was crucial to the well-being of their nation—and of the world at large. Try as he might, Johnson was having a hard time selling that same argument when it came to Vietnam. Seemingly undaunted, he assured his audience, "We will not be defeated. We will not grow tired. We will not withdraw."[37] Nor would he would go back on the promises that his predecessors, Presidents Eisenhower and Kennedy, had made to South Vietnam. A little over a year later, during a speech to Democrats in Chicago, Johnson accused critics of the war in Vietnam of effeminacy and disloyalty, similar to charges that were leveled nearly seventy years earlier against those who opposed the war in the Philippines. He told the audience, "There will be some Nervous Nellies who will become frustrated and bothered and break ranks under the strain."[38] Some of these individuals, Johnson added, "will turn on their own leaders and their own country, and on their own fighting men."[39]

Then, speaking at the University of Virginia's Miller Center on September 29, 1967, Johnson repeated many of his earlier arguments for why the United States had to continue to fight in Vietnam. Again, the president styled the conflict as one against outside Communist aggressors who were "ruthlessly attempting to bend a free people to its will." But Johnson assured his listeners the United States and its South Vietnamese allies had now turned the corner and were winning the war: "The military victory almost within Hanoi's grasp in 1965 has now been denied them. The grip of the Vietcong on the people is being broken."[40]

Much of what Johnson was saying in his speeches and other pronouncements to justify the war was untrue: The Munich analogy made no sense when applied to Southeast Asia, since Vietnam was not Nazi Germany and the conflict there was not another World War II. Nor was Vietnam the victim of "outside aggression"; rather, it was fighting for independence and self-determination. And critics of the war could not be dismissed as mere "Nervous Nellies." The true story of Vietnam was much more complex.

In fact, Johnson himself may not have believed all that he was saying in these speeches. As far back as March 1965, he had agreed during a conversation with his old friend Sen. Richard Russell of Georgia that there seemed no way to win in Vietnam. "We are losing more [men] every day," he admitted to Russell. "We're getting in worse. A man can fight if he can see daylight down the road somewhere, but there ain't no daylight in Vietnam. There's not a bit."[41] That summer, Johnson expressed similarly pessimistic thoughts about the war to his wife, Lady Bird Johnson: "Vietnam is getting worse every day. I have the choice to go in with great casualty lists or to get out with disgrace. It's like being in an airplane, and I have to choose between crashing the plane or jumping out. I do not have a parachute."[42] Despite his serious reservations, Johnson continued to believe China was pulling the strings in Vietnam as part of a wider conspiracy to dominate all of Asia. At the same time, he did not want to be the first president to lose a war, and he was afraid his critics would call him soft on Communism, as they had done to Truman.

At the very time Johnson was escalating the war, he was pushing hard for what became the Voting Rights Act of 1965, which sent federal registrars into southern states to ensure African Americans could finally exercise their right to register and vote. In a stirring speech before a joint session of Congress, Johnson proclaimed basic American rights for all people: "This was the first nation in the history of the world to be founded with a purpose—'Government by consent of the governed.' 'Give me liberty or give me death. . . .' It says that he shall share in freedom, [and] he shall choose his leaders."[43] Ho Chi Minh had uttered similar sentiments when he proclaimed Vietnam's independence at the end of World War II. Even if Johnson knew that, he continued to insist only the United States could free the Vietnamese, even as the Vietnamese fought to define their own future.

A person in government who well understood the Vietnamese drive for independence and self-determination was J. William Fulbright, chair of the Senate Foreign Relations Committee. In 1966, he gave a series of lectures criticizing the Vietnam War that were published in book form early the next year and entitled *The Arrogance of Power*. Fulbright was a dedicated internationalist, an early supporter of the United Nations, and a strong believer in international exchanges of students and scholars, which led him to sponsor what came to be called the Fulbright fellowships and scholars programs.

He was also an early and outspoken opponent of Joseph McCarthy and others in Congress who engaged in Communist witch hunts.

Fulbright's book was wide-ranging and insightful. He placed the larger Cold War into the contexts of both history and psychology, arguing that humanity must learn from both if the scourge of war is ever to be brought under meaningful control. Among the lessons he had learned from extensive reading and his many years as a member of the Foreign Relations Committee was the importance of under-standing cultures that are different from one's own, as opposed to arrogantly demonizing them because of their differences. Another lesson was the importance of making peace settlements "based on accommodation," as opposed to insisting on total victory; settle-ments made without compromise, wrote Fulbright, "have proven to be unstable, making for renewed conflict and generating greater problems than they solved."[44]

As applied to Vietnam, these lessons required understanding and appreciating that it was not possible in any foreseeable time for the United States to implant American-style democracy among a people who had no experience with it. The United States also needed to appreciate that China was, in fact, fearful of the American presence in Vietnam, especially given the United States' incessant demoniza-tion of China, including loud threats of nuclear attack, ever since the Chinese Communist Revolution of 1949. The solution for Vietnam, according to Fulbright, was a negotiated settlement among all parties that would lead to the neutralization of all Southeast Asia. Then the Vietnamese people themselves could decide, through internation-ally supervised elections, whom they wanted to govern them—a plan that had been mandated by the Geneva Accords a decade earlier and had been sabotaged by the Eisenhower administration. Above all, Fulbright charged that the current American policy of bombing and sending more and more troops into Vietnam would not cause the Vietnamese Communists, both North and South, to give up and cave in to the American demands.

In February 1966, the same year his book appeared, Fulbright, as head of the Senate's Foreign Relations Committee, launched the first series of televised hearings on the war in Vietnam. Unlike Henry Cabot Lodge, who had been chair of the same committee during the

Philippine War, Fulbright did not attempt to shield the president of his own party, Lyndon Johnson, from criticism. Among Fulbright's star witnesses was George Kennan, the author of the doctrine of containment and the most highly regarded foreign policy analyst of the era, who appeared before a closed hearing. In Kennan's opinion, the United States should withdraw from Vietnam "as soon as this could be done without inordinate damage to our prestige or stability in the area" in order to avoid the risk of war with China.[45]

Johnson took both the Fulbright hearings and Fulbright's book as personal attacks, especially since the senator had been one of the president's old friends. He simply could not accept that Fulbright's questioning of the war was the result of his sincere concern for the country. Johnson privately wondered if Fulbright had also become a dupe of the Communists and asked Federal Bureau of Investigation (FBI) director J. Edgar Hoover to see if any remarks made at the hearings appeared to be Communistic.[46] (This directive was not unlike Secretary of War Root's order to the commanding general in the Philippines to find out if any of the anti-imperialists had had contact with Filipino rebels.) Johnson and Fulbright managed to remain on speaking terms, but, during a one-on-one meeting, Johnson harangued Fulbright about his vow to use whatever force was necessary to make the Vietnamese Communists sit down at the negotiating table. Fulbright left the session shaken and told members of his staff back at the Capitol that he "was afraid the President was beyond a rational discussion of Vietnam."[47]

Historian Eric Goldman, who attended an informal discussion at the White House in 1966 with Johnson and several aides, came back from the meeting both incredulous and appalled at the president's accusation of Communist ties between antiwar senators and the Russians. According to Goldman, Johnson claimed that "the Russians were in constant touch with the anti-war senators—and he named names." These senators, in Johnson's telling, "ate lunch and went to parties at the Soviet embassy; children of their staff people dated Russians." Goldman quoted Johnson directly as saying, "The Russians think things up for the senators to say. I often know before they do what their speeches are going to say."[48]

And it was not just senators, the president believed, that Communists were attempting to influence, but everyone in government. In March 1966, Johnson insisted to an assemblage of state governors, "Our country is constantly under threat every day—Comm[unists] working every day to divide us, to destroy us." And these Communists were in "the highest counsels of gov[ernment]." He added, "McCarthy's methods were wrong—but the threat is greater now than in his day."[49] Mentally, Johnson seemed to be slipping back to the early days of the Cold War.

Another target of Johnson's wrath was Sen. Robert Kennedy, brother of the slain John F. Kennedy. Johnson had always disliked the Kennedys and particularly despised "Bobby," whom he had often referred to as "that little piss ant." At a meeting in the White House, where Kennedy laid out his ideas for a negotiated peace in Vietnam, Johnson exploded, saying, "I'll destroy you and every one of your dove friends in six months."[50]

Johnson was also incensed over increasing media criticism about the war. In December 1966, Harrison E. Salisbury, the assistant managing editor of the *New York Times*, launched a series of articles about how the American bombing of North Vietnam was killing and maiming civilians. The administration had insisted they were only targeting military and industrial sites, but Salisbury produced evidence to show large numbers of civilians were being seriously hurt or killed in the bombardments. The upshot was that the administration was continuing to hide the truth about the war, and Johnson was all the more furious because he knew the reporting was true.[51]

Johnson was not above asking the FBI to investigate journalists who reported sensitive information about the war. When Peter Lisagor of the *Chicago Daily News* revealed in June 1965 that the Russians had sent some medium-range bombers to North Vietnam, Johnson asked the FBI to find out who had given Lisagor his information. The bureau turned up nothing. The president also became convinced members of the media who reported negative information about the war were Communists. When R. W. Apple of the *New York Times* wrote from Saigon in August 1967 that the war had become a "stalemate," Johnson privately denounced him to a White House aide as a Communist.[52]

Not surprisingly, Johnson also accused antiwar demonstrators of

being Communists—or at least Communist inspired. These demonstrations coincided with a wider protest against the norms of postwar
American society known as the counterculture. There were demonstrations for black civil rights, women's rights, and free speech
on college campuses, among numerous other issues. Many of the
antiwar protests stemmed from opposition to the military draft,
which was administered unfairly, given that African Americans and
other minorities were far more likely to be conscripted than white,
middle-class youth. As the war went on, opposition to the draft also
emerged out of the belief the war itself was immoral. The first orga-
nized protest against the draft took place in New York in May 1964,
when about a dozen young men burned their draft cards. "Teach-
ins," the first taking place at the University of Michigan in March
1965, were held on numerous campuses thereafter. During these
events, speakers, including antiwar faculty, gave talks and led discussions about why the war was wrong. There were also mass marches
in various cities, especially in Washington, DC. On October 15, 1969,
hundreds of thousands skipped classes or called in sick to work in the
cause of a National Moratorium against the war.[53]

Although the bulk of antiwar protesters were young, Americans
of all ages and from all walks of life participated in demonstrations.
These included members of the League of Women Voters, Artists
and Writers Against the War in Vietnam, Women for Peace, and
the Catholic Workers Movement as well as Catholic nuns and clergy
from many denominations. The latter included the Reverend Doctor
Martin Luther King Jr., the widely acknowledged leader of the black
civil rights movement. During his speech at New York's Riverside
Church on April 4, 1967, to a group called Clergy and Laymen Concerned about Vietnam, he made a powerful call for sanity and justice.
He spoke with great feeling "of the people who have been living
under the curse of war for almost three continuous decades now"
who "must see Americans as strange liberators—strange liberators
who helped the French to crush their country's fight for independence. Then because the United States assumed that the Vietnamese
people were not ready for independence, we again fell victim to the
deadly Western arrogance that has poisoned the international atmosphere for so long." And, King lamented, in that arrogance, "we may

have killed a million of them, mostly children. They wander into the towns and see thousands of the children, homeless, without clothes, running in packs on the streets like animals." This madness had to cease, King cried: "I speak as a child of God and brother to the suffering poor of Vietnam. I speak for those whose land is being laid waste, whose homes are being destroyed, whose culture is being subverted." And in answer to those who were saying the United States had to stay in Vietnam to defeat Communism, he declared, "Our greatest defense against communism is to take offensive action in behalf of justice. We must with positive action seek to remove those conditions of poverty, insecurity, and injustice, which are the fertile soil in which the seed of communism grows and develops."[54]

Johnson, in his self-delusion, continued to believe most of those protesting or speaking out against the war were tainted by Communism in one way or another, including King. At the president's request, the FBI gathered reams of information about supposed ties between Communists and protesters. Even those who were not directly under Communist influences, he charged, were giving emotional support to the enemy in Vietnam. In the aftermath of a march against the Pentagon on October 21, 1967, an angry Johnson vowed, "I'm not going to let the Communists take over this government. . . . I am not going to let 200,000 of these people [demonstrating] ruin everything for the 200 million Americans."[55] Although there was no evidence Communists were organizing and directing the protests, Johnson had to believe they were; otherwise, he would need to conclude that the demonstrations, which were enlisting millions of people nationwide, were in fact made up of sincere citizens who believed the war was a terrible mistake that had to end.

Johnson was also very angry to see that television network news programs, now more critical of the war, were giving extensive coverage to the protests, and he complained to various television executives about what he considered to be slanted news. The Vietnam War was, in fact, the first "televised war." And this coverage had a powerful effect on viewers. Approximately 90 percent of American homes now owned televisions, and this relatively new medium had become the major news source for about 60 percent of Americans.[56] What viewers "witnessed" of the Tet Offensive in late January and early February

1968 was especially graphic and shocking: they watched cities being bombed, terrified civilians running through the streets, and prisoners of war being shot by the South Vietnamese. It was also in the aftermath of Tet that CBS's Walter Cronkite, the most trusted news anchor in America at the time (known affectionately by many viewers as "Uncle Walter"), expressed serious doubts about the course of the war. At the end of a news special about Vietnam, broadcast on February 27, 1968, he said, "It seems now more certain than ever, that the bloody experience of Vietnam is to end in a stalemate. To say that we are closer to victory today is to believe in the face of the evidence, the optimists who have been wrong in the past."[57] Cronkite's words went a long way to confirm what was coming to be called the "credibility gap"—the difference between the administration's claims and what was increasingly clear about the realities in Vietnam.

In the aftermath of Tet, it became clear to even Johnson and his advisors that the United States really had no plausible military strategy for either winning the war or getting out of Vietnam without complete humiliation. There was incredibly irresponsible talk among the president's national security advisors of using nuclear weapons against North Vietnam, even if it meant having to take on China and the Soviet Union and very possibly starting a nuclear World War III. Meanwhile, protests against the war grew more and more massive. Then, concluding he could not win another term as president, Johnson announced on March 31, 1968, in a nationally televised address, that he would not seek the Democratic Party's nomination. He would spend the remainder of his term seeking to negotiate an end to the war.

CHAPTER 6

THE DEFEATED GIANT

"I speak as a child of God and brother to the suffering poor of Vietnam. I speak for those whose land is being laid waste, whose homes are being destroyed, whose culture is being subverted."
—Martin Luther King Jr.

In May 1968, President Johnson succeeded in starting peace talks, to be held in Paris. But the talks made no real progress before Johnson left office, and they would not result in a peace agreement until January 1973, nearly five years later, in what must be seen as an American defeat. During the time the talks were taking place, tens of thousands more people, both American and Vietnamese, would be killed and maimed. Revelations of American atrocities in Vietnam would further undermine support for the war in the United States and badly tarnish the nation's claims to moral exceptionalism. As if that were not enough, the Nixon administration's criminal behavior in response to critics of the war and to other perceived enemies of the administration would force President Nixon to resign from office and would leave the American people a lasting legacy of mistrust of government.

Taking advantage of Johnson's vulnerability on Vietnam was Robert Kennedy, the brother of the slain President John F. Kennedy. Just two weeks before Johnson's announcement that he would not seek reelection, Kennedy had entered the race for the Democratic nomination. He had become an outspoken critic of the Vietnam War and promised that, if elected, he would end American participation in that conflict. Also seeking the Democratic nomination was Vice President Hubert

Humphrey, who was handicapped by his association with what many had come to call "Johnson's war." In contrast, Kennedy seemed to be well on his way to becoming the Democratic nominee following his victory in the California primary held on June 4. However, late that night, Kennedy was shot and killed at the Ambassador Hotel in Los Angeles as he was making his way through the hotel's kitchen en route to a press conference elsewhere in the building. With Kennedy dead, Humphrey was a cinch for the nomination.

The Democrats' convention, held in Chicago in late August, turned out to be a disaster for the party. Outside the convention hall, Chicago police, assisted by the Illinois National Guard, attacked protesters, resulting in what many called a police riot. The violent melee was televised live, nationwide, with the result that many viewers, through guilt by association, blamed the Democrats for the rioters. The violence outside the convention floor also gave a perfect campaign theme for the Republican nominee, Richard Nixon, who promised to restore law and order in the country. Realizing the great unpopularity of the war, Nixon said he had a "secret plan" for ending it. Although leading Humphrey in the early polls, Nixon's numbers began to slip after Humphrey distanced himself from Johnson and the war. Some analysts believed if the campaign had lasted another ten days or so, Humphrey would have won. As it turned out, Nixon garnered 43.42 percent of the popular vote to Humphrey's 42.72 percent. Third-party candidate George Wallace won 8.6 percent. In the Electoral College, Nixon led Humphrey 301–191, while Wallace scored 46 electoral votes. The announcement of the so-called secret plan to end the war may well have helped to put Nixon over the top. But if Robert Kennedy, with his famous name and star power, had not been killed, it is very possible that Nixon never would have made it into the White House and the Vietnam War would have ended several years before it did.

Nixon knew very well when he took office that the Vietnam War was unwinnable. His national security advisor, Henry Kissinger, also knew it. Nixon did genuinely wish to get out of Vietnam, but he did not want to be seen as the president who lost the war, and he did not want the United States to leave Vietnam in ignominious defeat, which is why he talked again and again about "peace with honor." But like Johnson

before him, Nixon did not understand Ho Chi Minh and his determination to fight on no matter the cost. Nor would he accept Ho's
demand for both a military and a political settlement that would
require the United States to withdraw all its troops and clear the way
for him to take over all Vietnam. Because Nixon would not agree to
these terms, the killing continued for nearly his entire presidency.
When he took office in January, more than thirty thousand Americans had lost their lives some ten thousand miles away from home.
By the time the war finally ended in defeat, nearly twice that number
of Americans had died in what had long been a futile commitment.

In an effort to persuade both China and the Soviet Union to
put pressure on the Vietnamese Communists to negotiate an end
of the war that would allow the United States to save face, Nixon
and Kissinger came up with the idea of "triangulation." During the
1950s and 1960s, China and the Soviet Union had diverged and
even argued over correct Communist ideology. In the late 1960s,
they began feuding with each other over the boundary between the
two countries, which devolved into actual shooting. This Sino-Soviet
split, as it was called, put into serious question the oft-stated assertion in the United States that Communism was monolithic and that,
therefore, China and the Soviet Union were engaged in a joint conspiracy against the West. In any case, the deepening split suggested to
Nixon and Kissinger that the United States could exploit Sino-Soviet
differences to seek better relations with both countries and induce
them to put pressure on the Vietnamese to agree to negotiations that
would allow the United States to save face.

Nixon astounded many on both the right and left when he
announced plans for a visit to the People's Republic of China (that
is, Communist China) in February 1972. Over the years, he had
been a leading anti-Communist and had vehemently opposed any
move to recognize "Red China." Nixon's talks with Mao Zedong
(also spelled Mao Tse-tung) and foreign minister Zhou Enlai (Chou
En-lai) did not lead immediately to diplomatic recognition, but the
United States promised to withdraw its forces from Taiwan and to
accept, in principle, that Taiwan was part of China. The talks led to
further dialogue between the two countries, and in 1978, the United
States extended full diplomatic recognition to the People's Republic,

nearly three decades after Mao's victory over Chinese Nationalist Chiang Kai-shek. Nixon realized full well that no Democrat could have made this move toward China, but he, with impeccable credentials as an anti-Communist, would be above suspicion and reproach. As Nixon said to Mao, "Those on the right can do what those on the left can only talk about."[1] In fact, if a Democratic president had even mentioned such a mission to China, Nixon himself would have surely excoriated him for being soft on Communism—or worse.

There were concerns that the Soviets would take the Chinese trip as a calculated slight, which, in fact, Nixon wanted them to do. Consequently, the Soviets invited Nixon to come to Moscow for a summit in May 1972, with the main goal of agreeing to the Strategic Arms Limitation Treaty. Nixon and Communist Party secretary Leonid Brezhnev agreed to recognize the status quo in Berlin, which for a quarter century had been a flash point, opening the way for the East and West German governments to sign treaties recognizing each other and formally assenting to the division of Germany. The diplomatic establishment as well as the news media used the word *détente* to label these better relations between East and West.

Nixon's visit to China and his agreements with the Soviet Union in 1972 were extraordinary achievements that, less than two decades later, would help to end the Cold War. But Nixon's triangulation did not immediately help to stop the Vietnam conflict. Meanwhile, continued revelations about the war stoked the opposition at home. In November 1969, some ten months after Nixon assumed the presidency, came the sickening news of a massacre by Americans troops at the Vietnamese village of My Lai (also known as Son My). The massacre had taken place on March 16, 1968, a month and a half after the Tet Offensive began, and was part of a larger search and destroy mission that would allow American forces to restore the initiative in South Vietnam. Although the massacre had taken place while Johnson was still president, public knowledge of it occurred on Nixon's watch.

My Lai actually referred to a cluster of villages that were allegedly held by the Communists. Col. Oran K. Henderson, commander of the Eleventh Brigade, told his officers to go into the area "aggressively, close with the enemy, and wipe them out for good." One of the officers, Capt. Ernest Medina, was quoted as saying, "They're all VC [Viet Cong], now go and get them . . . anybody that was running from us, hiding from us, or who appeared to be the enemy."[2] Units had also been ordered by Lt. Col. Frank A. Barker to "burn the houses, kill the livestock, destroy food supplies, and destroy the wells."[3] (The orders were hauntingly similar to those given on Samar in the Philippines nearly seventy years before: "I want no prisoners. I wish you to kill and burn: the more you kill and burn, the better you will please me [and] make Samar a howling wilderness."[4])

Those carrying out the raid at My Lai on March 18 seemed to interpret their orders to mean they should kill everyone in sight. One witness who testified during a court-martial for the prosecution recalled, "A lot of women had thrown themselves on top of the children to protect them, and the children were alive at first. Then the children who were old enough to walk got up and Lt. William Calley began to shoot the children."[5] Later sworn testimony revealed that some American troops that day had raped a number of young girls and women and then killed them.

The testimony of Private First Class Michael Bernhardt, who had come upon the scene while it was underway, was equally horrifying:

> I walked up and saw these guys doing strange things. . . . Setting fire to the hooches and huts and waiting for people to come out and then shooting them. . . . I saw them shoot an M79 [grenade launcher] into a group of people who were still alive. But it was mostly done with a machine gun. They were shooting women and children just like anybody else. We met no resistance and I only saw three captured weapons. We had no casualties. It was just like any other Vietnamese village—old papa-sans, women and kids. As a matter of fact, I don't remember seeing one military-age male in the entire place, dead or alive.[6]

Incredibly, an army photographer recorded the dead and dying, along with women and children fleeing in terror. Later, the photos appeared in full color in *Life* magazine, the same mass-circulation magazine that had published photographs three decades earlier of Japanese atrocities in Nanjing (Nanking), China.

Several American servicemen tried to stop the killing and even managed to rescue Vietnamese civilians. One of them was Warrant Officer Hugh Thompson Jr. Thompson was a helicopter pilot flying over the scene when he and his crew saw dead and wounded civilians on the ground. They landed near a ditch filled with dead and dying Vietnamese. When Thompson asked a sergeant at the site if he would help lift the people out of the ditch, the response was that he would "help [put] them out of their misery." A bit later, Thompson and his men spotted a group of children, women, and old men in a bunker who were being approached by a group of soldiers. Thompson landed and asked an American lieutenant to help extricate them. In Thompson's words, the lieutenant responded "that the only way to get them out was with a hand grenade." The crew, with help from a second helicopter, managed to rescue twelve civilians and fly them to safety. Thompson also ordered his men to fire on any of the American soldiers who tried to stop the rescue.[7]

Returning to base, Thompson reported the massacre to his superiors. The initial response was to call off similar search and destroy missions, but the military still recorded the massacre as a military victory and held to that line for over a year. Captain Medina received a commendation for the action, and army authorities in Vietnam dismissed charges of a massacre by stating that only twenty civilians had been killed at My Lai, all by accident. Then, in March 1969, a year after the massacre, Specialist 5 Ronald L. Ridenhour, a former helicopter door gunner (now out of the service) who had not been at My Lai but had heard about it, sent a letter to thirty members of Congress asking them to investigate the atrocity. He had carefully gathered evidence by interviewing a number of men who had been at My Lai and who had observed the atrocities firsthand. Most of the lawmakers ignored the letter, but Congressman Morris "Mo" Udall of Arizona urged the House Armed Services Committee to ask the Pentagon to open an investigation. The My Lai story became public when Seymour Hersh, an independent investigative journalist, broke the story on November 12, 1969, with an article carried by the Dispatch News Service. This was then picked up and published by many newspapers and news magazines.

The army's provost marshal general's office charged Lieutenant

Calley with premeditated murder. Accused of related crimes were twenty-five other men. Of the twenty-six in total who were charged, only Calley was found guilty, in March 1971. Throughout his four-month trial, he repeatedly said he was only following orders, even though this defense had been rejected during the Nuremberg Trials of Nazi war criminals, as well as during the trials of Japanese war criminals following World War II.[8] Calley was sentenced to life in prison. Later, his sentence was reduced to twenty years, but after Calley served just three and a half years, Nixon's secretary of the army, Howard Callaway, paroled him.

Calley's own account, entitled *Lieutenant Calley: His Own Story* (1971), remains a chilling read. According to him, the American troops were told to deal with the Viet Cong by eliminating them: "I never met someone who didn't say it." As to killing infants, Calley said, "On babies everyone's really hung up. . . . Of course, we've been in Vietnam for ten years now. If we're in Vietnam another ten, if your son is killed by those babies you'll cry at me, 'Why didn't you kill those babies that day?'" He went on to insist his actions in Vietnam did not bother him at all: "Killing those men in My Lai didn't haunt me. . . . We weren't in My Lai to kill human beings, really, we were there to kill ideology. . . . To destroy Communism." He even believed what he and the others had done was justified by what God had said to Saul in the Bible about the Amalekites (1 Samuel 15:3): "Now go and utterly destroy all that they have, and spare them not; but slay both man and woman, infant and suckling, ox and sheep, camel and ass." As Saul had obeyed God, Calley, by analogy, believed that he had only carried out what his country had commanded: "Personally, I didn't kill any Vietnamese that day: I mean personally. I represented the United States of America. My country." Especially shocking was the cavalier way he dismissed the rape of Vietnamese women and girls at My Lai: "In the other platoon," he related, "a GI raped a girl, another was in her mouth, another was in her hand, soldiers say . . . 'She waved goodbye.' Well I guess a lot of girls would rather be raped than be killed anyway."[9]

Comments about Calley made in 1972 by historian Jay Baird, the editor of a book of readings entitled *From Nuremberg to My Lai,* are worth repeating for the light they shed, not only on the massacre but also on all the tragedies and contradictions of the Vietnam War:

A nation which had prided itself on being the bearer of culture, democracy, and all that was good in the world suddenly found itself two decades after Nuremberg fighting a war that could not be won. . . . It came as a shock to many people when it was revealed during the course of the Calley court-martial that Americans were just as capable of committing mass murder as were the Fascists and Communists before them. . . . The Calley memoirs are an extraordinary document: they reveal the thoughts of the "boy next door" who went to war for America in the 1960s.[10]

Still, the military consistently described the massacre as an aberration—not at all typical of American behavior toward Vietnamese civilians. In fact, My Lai was anything but an aberration, according to journalist Nick Turse's meticulous investigations four decades later, which formed the basis for his best-selling 2013 book, *Kill Anything That Moves*.[11] Turse based his book on copious records in the US National Archives that had been compiled by the Vietnam War Crimes Working Group, whose investigations had taken place in secret and whose findings had never been made public. He also interviewed approximately one hundred men who had either participated in or witnessed war crimes in Vietnam. Based on such evidence, Turse wrote,

The stunning scale of civilian suffering in Vietnam is far beyond anything that can be explained as merely the work of some "bad apples," however numerous. Murder, torture, rape, abuse, forced displacement, home burnings, specious arrests, imprisonment without due process—such occurrences were a daily fact of life throughout the years of the American presence in Vietnam.

In addition, Turse reported, the files of the War Crimes Working Group revealed that members of every major army unit in Vietnam had committed atrocities against civilians—"*every* infantry, cavalry, and airborne division, and every separate brigade that deployed." These crimes, he charged, "were the inevitable outcome of deliberate policies, dictated at the highest levels of the military."[12] Among them was the use of daily body counts to measure alleged progress in the war. This measurement had the full backing of Defense Sec-retary McNamara, whose economics and business background had caused him to rely heavily on mathematical data and statistics. As applied to Vietnam, in Turse's words, "The statistically minded war managers focused, above all, on the notion of achieving a 'crossover point': the moment when American soldiers would be killing more enemies than their Vietnamese opponents could replace."[13] At that point, the Pentagon planners expected that Communist forces in Vietnam would give up the fight. But the Vietnamese did not look at the war in terms of a balance sheet; instead, they vowed to fight for their independence for as long as it took and regardless of the costs.

As a consequence of these mistaken American policies and assumptions, units were congratulated and rewarded for how many Vietnamese they killed. Although they were supposed to kill only enemy combatants, there was a great temptation to count any civil-ians they killed, purposely or not. This was because reporting high body counts meant rapid promotions for officers and various rewards for even the lowest-ranking soldiers, who could expect several days of rest and relaxation at the beach or other perks.

The declaration of free-fire zones further contributed to the civilian death toll. These were zones where the US Army believed that inhabitants were harboring Viet Cong fighters, and, as a result, American troops were authorized to attack any villages or individ-uals that were even slightly suspect. Often, mistakes were made, and totally innocent settlements that were either neutral or loyal to the Saigon government were destroyed and their inhabitants killed. In other cases, the residents had been forced to harbor Viet Cong fighters. Then there was the matter of terrified American troops who, in jungle terrain, could not tell who was friendly or not, leading them to fire at anyone they thought might be menacing.

Reducing qualms about killing civilians was the nearly universal racism and contempt the American forces exhibited toward all Viet-namese. The most common racial slur was to call the Vietnamese "gooks." The Americans also called them "slopes" or "slants." The latter referred to the shape of their eyes, while "gook" was probably a transmogrified form of "goo-goo," a term Americans had used for Fili-pinos during the Philippine War (and later toward other peoples they considered inferior)—yet another telling connection between these two tragic conflicts. American troops in Vietnam regularly described the country with such phrases as "the outhouse of Asia," "the garbage dump of civilization," "the asshole of the world."[14] All of this was another way of saying the Vietnamese were less than human. They were not entitled to basic human rights, and therefore, raping, killing, or torturing them was, for some soldiers, not at all remarkable or reprehensible. It is also likely the verbal denigration of Vietnam and the Vietnamese people represented the displaced anger of draftees who wanted to be anywhere other than where they were.

None of the higher-ranking officers who encouraged high body counts were ever held accountable. Nor did government officials back in Washington have to answer for initiating these policies. Even so, individual soldiers were expected to act in accordance with the international rules of war and with their own military's rules of engagement, which prohibited the intentional killing or harming of civilians. The great majority of the three million individual Americans who fought in Vietnam did conduct themselves properly and with honor. But those who did not do so seriously compromised the country they represented and inflicted hideous, unnecessary suffering on a people who only wanted independence and self-determination—values Americans had long cherished and proclaimed to the world.

Eighteen months after the My Lai revelations had slammed against the crumbling bulwarks of support for the war came the publication by the *New York Times*, beginning on June 13, 1971, of an internal study of the conflict, popularly called the Pentagon Papers. Secretary McNamara and President Kennedy had initially requested this inquiry, which had only recently been completed. The documents were officially entitled *United States-Vietnam Relations, 1945–1967: A Study Prepared by the Department of Defense.* This secret study had been turned over to the *Times* by Daniel Ellsberg, then an employee of the RAND Corporation. Among the most damning observations made in the document was that four presidential administrations—those of Truman, Eisenhower, Kennedy, and Johnson—had misled the public about their intentions in Vietnam and had painted falsely optimistic pictures about the progress of the war. These deceptions included schemes to provoke North Vietnam into launching a major military strike that would justify widespread retaliation by the United States. The papers also revealed that the Johnson administration had incorrectly justified the war as necessary for "containing" China and stopping it from organizing "all Asia against the United States." (It had not seemed to register with those in charge of American foreign policy that Ho Chi Minh would no more tolerate Chinese domination than he would domination by the United States—or, before that, domination by France or Japan.) Most damning of all was the indisputable proof that four administrations in a row had misled, dissembled, and outright lied in order to sell the war to the Congress and the public at large. These revelations could not be dismissed as the ravings of some crackpot dissenters or Communist-inspired protesters; they had come from the military establishment itself.

Initially, Nixon was not troubled by the publication of the Pentagon Papers because they dealt with Vietnam during the years before his presidency, but Kissinger convinced him that not prosecuting Ellsberg would set a dangerous precedent for protecting government secrets in the future. The Justice Department accordingly charged Ellsberg with violating the Espionage Act of 1917, but he was acquitted in a mistrial. Also unsuccessful were suits to stop the *New York Times* and other newspapers from publishing the Pentagon Papers.

The Nixon administration decided to take the law into its own hands to discredit Ellsberg and anyone else who had leaked information from the government. The White House authorized the "Plumbers" unit, so named because its mission was to "plug" such leaks to the media. The group was established July 24, 1971, and financed by the Committee to Re-elect the President. The Plumbers broke into the office of Ellsberg's psychiatrist and pried open a filing cabinet to find evidence they could use against Ellsberg. During Nixon's reelection campaign in 1972, the Plumbers conducted a host of illegal activities on behalf of the Committee to Re-elect. These included breaking into the Democratic Party headquarters in Washington's Watergate complex to install electronic listening devices so that Nixon's campaign could discover the Democrats' plans. The Plumbers were caught by a security guard when they returned to the Watergate to replace a defective listening device. President Nixon personally authorized bribes to keep the men from revealing their connections with the administration and otherwise managed a "cover-up" of what came to be called the Watergate scandal. The scandal would eventually force Nixon to resign from office rather than face certain impeachment by the House of Representatives and conviction by the Senate.

Meanwhile, the war went on. When Nixon took office, some two hundred Americans were dying each week, and he realized he would have to do something or face the wrath of antiwar groups. His "secret plan," to which he had referred toward the end of the campaign, was "Vietnamization," whereby American troops would be pulled out and replaced by South Vietnamese units. He initiated the plan in March 1970 by announcing he would bring 150,000 troops home the following year. Predictably, as more and more American troops were pulled out and it looked increasingly likely that the Communists were winning, Nixon responded with savage bombing of North Vietnam, the destruction of dams, and the mining of Haiphong Harbor. In fact, Nixon wanted the Chinese, the Soviets, and the North Vietnamese to think he had gone crazy and would stop at nothing to win the war. Journalist and historian Marvin Kalb recalled that senior State Department officials were purposely telling reporters such things as "Nixon has gone mad" and "No one can control him any more—he's nuts."[15]

While this was happening, the peace talks, which had been initiated by Johnson after he decided not to seek another term in 1968, were continuing to take place in Paris. Nixon hoped his hard line on Vietnam would force the North Vietnamese negotiators to see reason, but they demanded a unilateral withdrawal of American troops and the destruction of the South Vietnamese regime as a precondition for serious talks. Nixon refused these demands from what he called that "little shit ass country."[16] In March 1969, he ordered the bombing of Communist supply lines in neighboring Cambodia. Realizing these air raids would provoke a new wave of antiwar demonstrations, Nixon ordered the operations to take place in secret.

In April 1970, the president again ordered attacks on Communist forces in Cambodia—this time, with American and South Vietnamese ground forces. This time, also, he announced his decision over nationwide television. He chose the White House map room for the announcement in order to associate himself with other wartime presidents: "In this room," he told the television audience, "Woodrow Wilson made the great decisions which led to victory in World War I. Franklin Roosevelt made the decisions which led to our victory in World War II. Dwight D. Eisenhower made decisions which ended the war in Korea and avoided war in the Middle East. John F. Kennedy, in his finest hour, made the great decision which removed Soviet nuclear missiles from Cuba and the Western Hemisphere."[17] Besides associating himself with these presidents, Nixon was trying to claim the war in Vietnam was on the same level of importance as World War I, World War II, the Korean War, and the threat of nuclear conflict during the Cuban Missile Crisis.

Nixon insisted he was seeking not to widen the war but to end it more quickly by eliminating Communist supply lines in Cambodia. Above all, the United States had to stay the course in Vietnam; otherwise, American credibility would be permanently damaged around the globe. In a reference to both the domino theory and the Munich analogy, the president warned, "If, when the chips are down, the world's most powerful nation, the United States of America, acts like a pitiful, helpless giant, the forces of totalitarianism and anarchy will threaten free nations and free institutions throughout the world."[18] It was 1938 again, and he, Richard Nixon, was not going to be another Neville Chamberlain.

Major media sources did not accept Nixon's justifications for the Cambodian invasion. In a front page editorial, the *New Republic* proclaimed, "Richard Nixon is going down in history all right, but not soon enough," adding that the speech was "insensitive," "phony," "a fraud," and "dangerous." The *New York Times* declared Nixon was "out of touch with the nation."[19]

The Cambodian decision also gave new life to the antiwar movement, which had been somewhat quiescent since Nixon had become president and promised to wind down the war. Campus protests broke out from one end of the country to the other. At Kent State University in Ohio, on May 4, panicky National Guard troops fired their rifles into a group of students, killing four and seriously wounding nine others. A week and a half later, on May 15, students were shot and killed at Mississippi's Jackson State University when police fired into a women's dormitory. Students across the nation reacted in fury,

occupying administration buildings, boycotting classes, and demon-
strating wherever they could. Many colleges simply closed for the
balance of the semester to avoid further violence and upheaval.

There was also growing opposition to the war in Congress. Legislators responded by requiring American troops to withdraw from
Cambodia within thirty days, the first formal and effective move by
legislators to limit the war in Southeast Asia. Despite Congress's clear
opposition to widening the conflict, Nixon ordered American air
support for a South Vietnamese invasion of Laos in February 1971.
Then, in October 1972, the North Vietnamese, acting under pressure from the Soviets, signaled their willingness to resume serious
talks. Negotiators in Paris agreed that the remaining sixty thousand
American troops would leave Vietnam, with Communist forces maintaining their current positions in the field, while South Vietnamese
president Nguyen Van Thieu would remain in power for the time
being. Thieu rejected the peace plan, and Nixon resumed heavy
bombing over Christmas 1972. In January 1973, both sides finally
accepted an agreement that was little different from the one proposed in October, and American participation in the Vietnam War
finally came to an end. More than fifty-eight thousand Americans
had died and more than three hundred thousand were wounded in
what was the nation's longest war at the time. About a million Vietnamese were killed and millions made homeless.[20]

It was only a matter of time until the Communists triumphed in
South Vietnam. In April 1975, Saigon fell to North Vietnamese and
Viet Cong forces. The United States had clearly lost a war that had
been unwinnable from the beginning and that it never should have
fought. The fate of Vietnam had nothing to do with American security or with genuine American national interests. From beginning to
end, it was a highly political war, since none of the presidents in power
during the Vietnam years, including President Eisenhower, wanted to
be accused of losing Vietnam. But the Democrats, in particular, knew
it would be political suicide to pull out and face a firestorm of accusations from the Republicans that they were soft on Communism.

The war also brought down two presidents. Johnson was forced
to give up running again in 1968 because of his close association
with a war gone disastrously wrong. The lies both Nixon and Johnson

had told about winning the Vietnam War, combined with Nixon's repeated lying about his role in the Watergate scandal, created a mistrust and cynicism about government that remains nearly half a century later.

Nixon's successor, Vice President Gerald R. Ford, had thoroughly supported the war in Vietnam. As a member of the House of Representatives, he had been an outspoken critic of President Johnson for not prosecuting the conflict more vigorously; he had accused the president on the floor of the House of not having a plan to win the war. In 1965, he joined, as House Minority Leader, with Republican Senate Minority Leader Everett Dirksen of Illinois to take Johnson to task in a series of popular televised press conferences that were soon dubbed the "Ev and Jerry Show." These joint appearances were calculated by the Republican Party to criticize Johnson's policies, including charges he was not doing enough to secure victory in Vietnam. Criticisms of Johnson for not prosecuting the war more forcefully were doubtless sincere, but they were also part of a larger political strategy of the Republicans to discredit the administration and score points for the party.

Ford's first important decision as president was to pardon Nixon for any crimes he may have committed regarding the Watergate scandals. Ford justified this decision by saying he had been able to do little else in his first month as president besides answering questions about whether or not the former president would be prosecuted for Watergate. The pardon decision touched off a firestorm of protest. Detractors charged that Nixon and Ford had made a deal in which Nixon agreed to resign in exchange for a pardon—a contention that Ford strenuously denied and for which there is no documented evidence. Others pointed to the seeming hypocrisy of sparing Nixon while refusing pardons for Vietnam War draft resisters. Still others claimed there was a double standard of justice: common lawbreakers felt the full force of the law, while Nixon, who had subverted the Constitution, received special treatment. These criticisms would continue throughout Ford's two years and four months as president and may well have deprived him of winning a term in his own right in 1976.

When Ford entered the presidency, there was much less drama in foreign affairs. Absent were the historic summits of the Nixon years.

At the same time, there was an exaggerated sense that the United States had lost much of its global power and the country's most glorious days were somehow over. More than anything else, the American defeat in Vietnam revealed the limits of the country's ability to work its will in the world when it came to military power. This may have been one reason Ford hung on to some hope the United States could still prevail in Vietnam. Despite the fact that the Saigon government had little hope of maintaining power after Congress passed the Case-Church bill of June 1973 that cut off all funds for the war, Ford promised South Vietnam's President Thieu that US commitments made to his country remained valid and would be fully honored by his administration.

Ford continued to make such assurances and to petition Congress for aid to the beleaguered Thieu until days before Saigon fell to the Communists, knowing full well that the legislators would not comply and thereby escaping any blame for himself. Tellingly, just a week before, in a speech at Tulane University, Ford had admitted the war was lost: "Today, America can regain the sense of pride that existed before Vietnam. But it cannot be achieved by refighting a war that is finished as far as America is concerned."[21] It is not clear if Ford remembered the many times he had castigated Lyndon Johnson for not fighting hard enough to win the war—or if he had simply been forced by the sequence of events to change his views.

Meanwhile, it was becoming evident the rigid Cold War policies of the past three decades were less and less appropriate. Discredited was the theory of monolithic Communism. In Yugoslavia, Marshal Tito had practiced his own, independent brand of socialism, refusing to join the Soviet-led Warsaw Pact or to become a puppet of the Kremlin. Nor had the victory of Communism in China led to a cozy relationship with the Soviet Union. Instead, age-old animosities between the two nations had grown more pronounced. Furthermore, the victory of Communist forces in Vietnam did not make Indochina into a satellite of either China or the Soviet Union. The Communist takeover of Vietnam also failed to injure American interests in any way, and in 1995, the United States normalized relations with that country, leading to increasing trade between the two nations and even growing tourism by Americans to this former enemy country.

The United States might not have become a "pitiful, helpless giant," as Richard Nixon had warned it would if it gave up on Vietnam. But it did become a defeated giant, whose wounds were self-inflicted. It remained to be seen if future leaders would learn from this defeat and not make similarly disastrous errors in judgment.

CHAPTER 7

UNRAVELING IRAQ

"Wars break things, kill people, and leave in their
wake horrendous confusion, chaos, and physical and
social upheavals. . . . Religious, political, or ethnic
rivalries, kept under a lid before the invasion, may
erupt unpredictably in the invasion's aftermath. . . .
If you break it, you own it."

—Colin Powell

By the early 1990s, there was much talk in government circles, as well as in the public and the news media, about the peace dividends that would surely result from the end of the Cold War: Spending for the military could decrease; NATO could be expanded into Eastern Europe; exchanges of goods, money, people, and ideas could return to early twentieth-century channels before the two world wars had sabotaged an earlier global economy; and the United States could work closely with the Soviet Union (and then, Russia) to solve international problems. And in instances where the two superpowers might not agree, there seemed virtually no chance disagreements would explode into a nuclear war. Although Cold War conflicts came to an end, the George W. Bush administration launched a wholly needless war against Iraq in 2003, with deadly repercussions that have continued for more than a decade. Unfortunately, little or nothing had been learned from past disasters like the wars in the Philippines and Vietnam.

Before that, a new international landscape was evident during the closing years of the George H. W. Bush presidency (known as Bush 41) and throughout the Clinton administration that followed.

Unfortunately, President George W. Bush, son of the first President Bush (and called Bush 43) envisioned a new kind of cold war that culminated in a disastrous invasion of Iraq.

During the first Bush presidency, Soviet head of state Mikhail Gorbachev had given up an empire in exchange for what he continued to call a "common European home" and for his dream of a "new world order." Although Bush 41 was skeptical of Gorbachev at first, he was both heartened and amazed when, following Iraqi dictator Saddam Hussein's invasion of oil-rich Kuwait on August 2, 1990, the Soviets condemned this naked aggression, even though Iraq was one of its staunchest allies. The Soviet position gave Bush a free hand to come down hard on Iraq without fear of a dangerous confrontation with the Russians. On August 30, Bush used Gorbachev's term "new world order" during a press conference to explain his rationale for using force against the Iraqi invaders.

Bush's arguments for using force against the Iraqis were twofold: First, the United States needed to protect access to oil in the region, for itself as well as for its allies. Kuwait was a major oil supplier to the United States, and if Hussein moved through Kuwait into neighboring Saudi Arabia, he would control one-fifth of the world's oil reserves. Second, military action against the Iraqis would support the security and stability of friendly states in the Persian Gulf area and would give notice that aggression against the territory of sovereign nations would not be tolerated. Bush did not want to use force, but he warned the Iraqis he would have no other choice if they did not evacuate Kuwait. However, the United States would not act alone. Bush and his foreign policy team obtained a UN Security Council resolution authorizing the use of military assets against Iraq, which the Soviet Union supported. Bush went on to assemble an alliance of thirty-four nations, the largest coalition assembled since World War II, with the Saudis paying for much of the cost of the fighting.

After bombing Iraq for several weeks, coalition ground troops—the vast majority of them American—entered Kuwait and, after just one hundred hours, were able to push the Iraqis out of the country. Bush faced the dilemma of whether or not to pursue the Iraqis all the way to their capital at Baghdad, but he decided not to for fear many members of the coalition would not go along with a widening of the war. He also feared toppling Hussein's regime might well plunge Iraq into civil war—a very farsighted view, given what happened when his son, Bush 43, invaded Iraq a decade later with the goal of overthrowing the Iraqi government.

In the immediate aftermath of the Persian Gulf War, Bush 41's approval ratings reached stratospheric levels of about 90 percent (the highest ever recorded), only to tumble back to about 40 percent by the time he ran for a second term in November 1992. The reasons for this slide were his breaking a promise not to raise taxes, which angered many Republicans, and the high unemployment rates at the time of his bid for reelection. It also did not help that the sixty-eight-year-old Bush was facing off against the forty-six-year-old, charismatic Bill Clinton, a two-term governor of Arkansas whom the Democrats had tapped as their presidential candidate. Besides that, independent candidate Ross Perot took many votes that probably would have gone to Bush. Ironically, Bush had acted both responsibly and pragmatically in limiting the scope of the first Gulf War and in supporting a tax hike to deal with ballooning deficits, which were the result of deep tax cuts, along with huge increases in defense spending, during the preceding Reagan administration. Clinton won the election with forty-five million popular votes to Bush's thirty-nine million and Perot's eighteen million. The electoral count was 370 for Clinton, 168 for Bush, and none for Perot.

Although Clinton was of age to serve in Vietnam, he had avoided the draft through a series of deft but entirely legal strategies. He faced some criticism for not having served, but the widespread belief the Vietnam War had been a disastrous mistake, coupled with the end of the Cold War, caused enough voters to discount the fact that he was not a veteran.

With the Cold War over, Clinton believed he could concentrate mainly on domestic affairs, though there turned out to be a number of international issues that demanded his attention. In dealing with the Russians—no longer the Soviets after the dissolution of the Soviet Union in 1991—Clinton cultivated a personal relationship with Russian president Boris Yeltsin, who had replaced Gorbachev as leader of his country. "Bill and Boris," as the media dubbed them, met a total of eighteen times during the Clinton years, nearly as often as all their predecessors combined during the Cold War. Clinton offered Yeltsin considerable financial support to stabilize the Russian economy, as well as membership in the Global Group of Eight (G8, known as the G7 before Russia's inclusion), whose members represented the world's leading economies. Clinton and Yeltsin also worked to convince former Soviet republics, which were now independent, to abide by the same arms control agreements that had been signed by the United States and the former Soviet Union and to transfer any nuclear weapons within their jurisdictions to Russia. The United States then provided both financial and technical support to dismantle these weapons once they were under Russian control.

Clinton also had to deal with various issues involving Iraq. One was maintaining no-fly zones in the northern part of Iraq to keep Hussein's forces from bombing the Kurdish minorities living there and in the southern part of the country to protect the Shiites there from aerial assaults. In June 1993, Clinton ordered the launching of twenty-three cruise missiles from ships in the Persian Gulf against targets in Iraq in retaliation for the Iraqi Intelligence Service's attempt to assassinate former president George H. W. Bush during his visit to Kuwait earlier that year. In October of the following year, Clinton ordered the deployment of a variety of military forces near the Iraqi border in response to Hussein's sending some sixty-three thousand troops to the frontier with Kuwait. All these were measured responses that aimed to keep Iraq contained and unable to strike again at its neighbors. In 1998, Clinton signed congressional legislation known as the Iraq Liberation Act. The legislation stated, "It should be the policy of the United States to support efforts to remove the regime headed by Saddam Hussein from power in Iraq and to promote the emergence of a democratic government to replace that regime." However, the legislation did not urge or authorize the use of military force to accomplish this goal.

Iraq remained contained, but members of the Republican Party criticized Clinton for not using more military muscle against Iraq.

Clinton's vice president, Al Gore, received his party's nomination for president in 2000. The Republicans turned to George W. Bush. After college, Bush worked in the oil business and then became a co-owner of an American League baseball team, the Texas Rangers.

From 1995 to 2000, he was governor of Texas. Unlike his father, Bush 41, he had no experience with foreign policy. In addition, according to biographer Jean Edward Smith, the younger Bush was, according to his classmates at Harvard Business School, "dynamically ignorant." As Smith put it, "He was energetic, but ill-informed, untutored, and unread. And he flaunted [his ignorance]."[1] Bush also did not read newspapers, Smith observed, as many of his predecessors had done in order to be as informed as possible about what was happening in the country and the world—a failing that could only have deepened his ignorance and isolation.[2]

Although Bush lost the popular tally by more than half a million votes that November, he became president by narrowly winning a majority of the Electoral College (271–266). Disputed returns in Florida led to intervention by the US Supreme Court in the case *Bush v. Gore*, with the justices voting to stop the Florida recount and to agree with the state's attorney general to award Florida's twenty-five electoral votes to Bush.

Having lost the popular vote, Bush could not legitimately claim a strong mandate to govern, but he soon acted as if he did enjoy the overwhelming approval and support of the American people. His vice president, Richard "Dick" Cheney, particularly insisted they take on the mantle of a mandate and, in that way, force the Washington establishment, the media, and the American people to accept the administration as legitimate.

There has been much debate about the role Cheney played in the administration. Some critics have contended that Cheney was the real president and that the inexperienced Bush was a mere puppet in his hands. Such claims are an exaggeration, but, during his first term, Bush did lean heavily on Cheney for advice and direction, especially in foreign affairs. Cheney had served for more than ten years in the US House of Representatives, was White House chief of staff for two years under President Ford, and was secretary of defense under Bush 41. As a member of the Ford and the Bush 41 administrations, Cheney had not stood out as an extreme conservative, which led some observers to suppose he had changed in the years since. Bush 43's first secretary of state, Colin Powell, disagreed with this assessment, contending that Cheney, who was much younger and much less experienced than Ford or Bush 41, had been contained by these earlier presidents. In the words of journalist and historian Peter Baker, Cheney had been "surrounded by other adults in the room with experience and gravitas."[3]

Cheney and several key advisors belonged to a loosely knit group known as neoconservatives (neocons for short). These included I. Lewis "Scooter" Libby, Cheney's assistant for National Security Affairs; Secretary of Defense Donald Rumsfeld; Deputy Secretary of Defense Paul Wolfowitz; chair of the Defense Policy Advisory Board Richard Pearle; and Undersecretary for Defense Policy Douglas Feith.

The neocons had had their roots in the Cold War and the strong anti-Communist consensus of American liberals at that time. But when many liberals turned against the war in Vietnam, those who thought the country should continue to oppose Communism by force established what became the neoconservative movement. Once the Cold War ended, they wanted to use America's standing as the only remaining superpower to shape the world to their liking. In particular, they turned their attention to spreading democracy in authoritarian countries, even if it meant using military force, with the belief that democratic governments were less likely to go to war with each other and would be more sympathetic to the United Sates. While it may be true that democratic governments are less likely to go to war with each other, implanting democracy by force in countries where there was no tradition of it would prove to be a very difficult and dangerous matter.[4]

The neocons had had no success during the Bush 41 administration, since the moderate and widely experienced George H. W. Bush had little sympathy for their views. However, his son was a blank slate when it came to foreign policy, and the neocons in the George W. Bush administration scored significant successes in getting him to adopt their views.

Surprisingly, during the candidate debates in the 2000 presidential campaign, Bush had called for restraint in foreign policy: "I'm not so sure the role of the United States is to go around the world and say, 'This is the way it's got to be.' I just don't think it's the role of the United States to walk into a country and say, we do it this way, so should you. I think the United States must be humble and must be proud and confident of our values, but humble in how we treat nations that are figuring out how to chart their own course." He also warned against American arrogance: "If we're an arrogant nation, they'll resent us. If we're a humble nation, but strong, they'll welcome us. Our nation stands alone right now in the world in terms of power, and that's why we've got to be humble, and yet project strength in a way that promotes freedom. . . . We're a freedom-loving nation, and if we're an arrogant nation, they'll view us that way, but if we're a humble nation, they'll respect us."[5]

Bush's philosophy of foreign policy as presented during the debates was both impressive and commendable, representing the best possible approach in dealing with other nations: remain strong, show a good example to the rest of the world, and refrain from using military power unless it is absolutely necessary. Regrettably, Bush did not practice what he preached when he dragged the United States into one of the most disastrous wars in its history.

Some commentators have alleged that the reasons for this change were several. For one, possibly, Bush had spent his life trying to measure up to his famous father, with whom he had had a strained relationship over the years. One night, the younger Bush came to his parents' house drunk and bashed his car into a neighbor's trash can. When his father admonished him, he retorted, "You wanna go mano a mano right here?"[6] Bush was later upset when it became evident his father thought Jeb, the second Bush son, should become the second Bush president. Bush 43 was also critical of his father, saying Bush 41 had "cut and run" too early from Iraq during the Persian Gulf War. Once he told a media consultant, referring to his father's time in office, "Don't underestimate what you can learn from a failed presidency."[7] And in contrast to the East Coast–bred father, some White House aides liked to stress to reporters that the son hailed from west Texas and could cope with "the streets of Laredo." No one was going to call him a wimp, as *Newsweek* had labeled his father.[8]

A great foreign policy achievement would allow Bush 43 to best the senior Bush. He also wanted to go down in history as one of the country's greatest presidents. Throughout American history, what had often provided the opportunity for greatness in the presidency was a serious crisis such as the Civil War, the Great Depression, or World War II. The terrorist attacks on the United States on September 11, 2001, offered Bush such an opportunity. This is not to say Bush was insincere in wanting to protect the country from further such attacks and go after the perpetrators.

Tellingly, at the first meeting of the National Security Council, held at the White House on January 30, 2001, just ten days after Bush's inauguration, the group took up the subject of Iraq. Since the end of the Persian Gulf War of 1991, the United States had continued to enforce no-fly zones in both the northern and southern parts of Iraq, areas where the Iraqi air force was forbidden to operate. Economic sanctions had also been in place against Iraq, but the Iraqis had found ways to get around them. At the meeting, Secretary of State Powell suggested sanctions be tightened and better enforced. Secretary of Defense Rumsfeld responded by asking, "Why are we even bothering with sanctions?"[9] Far more important to Rumsfeld was locating and destroying weapons of mass destruction (WMD) he believed were still in Iraq. The president asked Powell to look into tightening sanctions and directed Rumsfeld to examine the military options for addressing the Iraqi situation.

The events of 9/11 are well known, including the two planes that were flown into the World Trade Center in New York City; a third plane that was flown into the Pentagon; and the crash of a fourth aircraft, United Airlines Flight 93, which was en route to Washington for an attack on the nation's capital. In total, nearly three thousand individuals were killed that day. Following these terrifying events, the neocons gained tremendous influence in the administration.

On the evening of September 11, Bush addressed the nation over live television. He proclaimed, "We are at war against terror." But being at war against an amorphous idea was difficult to grasp, which may partly explain why the president added, "We will make no distinction between the terrorists who committed these acts and those who harbored them."[10] Nine days later, during a speech to a joint session of Congress, the president repeated his declaration of a "war on terror." Not everyone was happy about Bush's use of the word *war*. US Senate Majority Leader Tom Daschle, a Democrat, objected at a White House meeting the next day, saying *war* was "a very powerful word" and adding, "This war is so vastly different [from more conventional conflicts]."[11] Besides, such a war might not result in any tangible victory, which would put both the president and the nation in a very difficult situation wherein failure to achieve an all-out victory could look like defeat.

Bush went further during his State of the Union message the following January 29 to denounce what he called an "axis of evil," whose members were Iran, Iraq, and North Korea. Bush accused all three of aiding terrorists and seeking "weapons of mass destruction," but he placed the greatest stress on the danger posed by Iraq.[12] Presidential speechwriter David Frum later admitted he had used the word *axis* very consciously as a way of comparing the nation's current enemies to the Axis powers of World War II (namely Germany, Japan, and Italy). An administration spokesperson later tried to qualify the phrase by saying the president had not intended to say that Iran, Iraq, and North Korea were actually collaborating with one another but that they were all doing the same evil things independently.[13]

Regardless of exactly what the president may have meant, "axis of evil" was also reminiscent of Ronald Reagan's denunciation back in 1983 of the Soviet Union as an "Evil Empire." The similarity in phrases was no accident, according to Michael Isikoff and David Corn in their book, *Hubris*, about the origins of the war in Iraq. According to them, "Ever since September 11, 2001, Bush had increasingly identified with Reagan: his optimism, his firm convictions, his stark, uncompromising stand against Communism."[14] As such, Bush envisioned a new Cold War—not against Communism this time but against Islamic extremism, since it was now clear Osama bin Laden's al-Qaeda network was behind the 9/11 attacks.

The Axis of Evil speech likely would not have been made were it not for the 9/11 attacks. Nor would the neocons in the administration have been able to insist on a war in Iraq to topple Saddam Hussein. One of their main arguments in favor of the war was what might be called a reverse domino theory: During the Cold War against Communism, the principal architects of American foreign policy had insisted Communism was bound to spread from one country to the next, like a row of falling dominoes, so that opposing attempted Communist takeovers, such as in Vietnam, was claimed to be essential for protecting the surrounding countries. Some people even had gone so far as to insist Americans had to fight Communism in Southeast Asia so they did not have to fight Communism at home. Now, so the argument went, the United States would implant democracy in Iraq, and it would spread from there throughout the Middle East, allowing the country to fight terrorism abroad instead of at home.[15]

Bush, Cheney, and the other neocons in the administration should have known better than to make this argument, since anyone who has taken a basic political science or history course should know political systems cannot be imposed easily from the outside. Instead, political systems evolve gradually out of the culture, traditions, and experiences of a people. This had been true of American democracy, whose roots went well back into the colonial period when there had been a substantial degree of representative government through the colonial legislatures. American democracy was also rooted in the centuries-old English common law and in various documents of British history, such as the Magna Carta of 1215 and the English Bill of Rights passed by Parliament in 1689. In this sense, the neocons were making the same mistake as Woodrow Wilson, who believed victory in World War I would cause democracy to spread quickly throughout large parts of the world.

Those who attempted to use the United States' implanting of democracy in Germany and Japan after World War II to prove its ability to do the same in Iraq were again ignorant of the historical record. Germany had experienced representative democracy before the Nazis took over, and many Germans were well aware of the various Western traditions of representative government. Although there was less of a democratic tradition in Japan, the country had made a written constitution in 1889 and created a bicameral legislature styled as a parliament and based on European models. Unfortunately, a largely autonomous Japanese military was able to use emergency powers provided for in the constitution to create a dictatorship in the 1920s.[16] Still, there was something of a template for the American occupation to establish a democratic government in Japan following World War II.

Then there were those in the Bush administration, such as Vice President Cheney and Secretary of Defense Rumsfeld, who boasted the Iraqis would welcome American intervention. On September 14, Cheney insisted to host Tim Russert on the television news program *Meet the Press,* "My belief is we will, in fact, be greeted as liberators."[17] As events would show, he could not have been more wrong.

But liberation and democracy arguments were not, initially, the main ones in the administration's campaign to convince Congress and the American people an invasion of Iraq was necessary. The administration alleged that (1) Iraq and its leader, Saddam Hussein, were closely linked to the 9/11 attacks, and (2) Iraq possessed WMDs that had to be seized and destroyed. The day after Bush gave his September 20 address to Congress, he wandered into the office of Richard Clarke, his counterterrorism chief. Clarke remembered being astounded when the president said, "I want you, as soon as you can, to go back over everything, everything. See if Saddam Hussein did this. See if he's linked in any way." When Clarke responded that the culprit was al-Qaeda, the president answered, "I know, I know, but see if Saddam was involved. Just look, I want to know any shred."[18] As it turned out, Hussein had nothing to do with the 9/11 attacks and did not possess weapons of mass destruction, but the administration did everything it could to make these cases.

During his speech to Congress on September 20, Bush also demanded the Taliban who controlled Afghanistan turn over to the United States the leaders of al-Qaeda and shut down their training camps. These demands, he added, were not open to discussion, and if they were not met, the Taliban would share the same fate as al-Qaeda. Congress had responded two days earlier to the attacks by authorizing the president "to use all necessary and appropriate force against those nations, organizations, or persons he determines planned, authorized, committed, or aided the terrorist attacks that occurred on September 11, 2001, or harbored such organizations or persons."[19] Some critics believed the statement was far too broad (as some critics had believed four decades earlier that the Gulf of Tonkin Resolution had been much too broad) and would allow the president to do almost anything as commander in chief. In any case, Bush convened a meeting with his defense team the day after the speech to plan an attack on Afghanistan.

The following day, September 22, the president held a cabinet meeting at the presidential retreat at Camp David in Maryland. At that meeting, assistant secretary of defense (and outspoken neocon) Paul Wolfowitz also began asserting the need to go to war against Iraq and Saddam Hussein. He declared that Afghanistan—the headquarters of al-Qaeda and the hideout of its leader, Osama bin Laden—would not be an especially attractive place for a war, since there were so few important targets in this primitive country. Iraq, in contrast, would have plenty of targets to hit.

Secretary of State Powell and National Security Advisor Condoleezza Rice were both irritated at Wolfowitz's suggestion. Voicing his dissent, Powell insisted, "No one will understand or support us doing anything but going after those who attacked us," adding that launching a military campaign against Iraq would shatter the coalition against al-Qaeda that the administration was trying to assemble. Rumsfeld retorted that maybe it was "not a coalition worth having." When Wolfowitz persisted in his campaign for an attack against Iraq, Bush broke in and said, "How many times do I have to tell you we are *not going* after Iraq right this minute?"[20] Later that day, Powell persisted in arguing Afghanistan should be the target: "Whatever problem Iraq is," he said, "it is not the cause of what happened [on 9/11]."[21] As it turned out, Powell was correct in his analysis: since al-Qaeda was based in Afghanistan, it made abundant sense to try to destroy the movement there. Unfortunately, a decision to invade Iraq two years later would seriously undermine progress against al-Qaeda in Afghanistan.

Although Bush did not think the time was right to go to war in Iraq, he clearly did not rule it out. Meanwhile, Vice President Cheney began searching for evidence that would justify an invasion of Iraq. When CIA analysts could not provide him with the evidence he wanted—because the facts were either very uncertain or lacking altogether—Cheney went personally to CIA headquarters and pushed analysts to find the "proofs" that he wanted. The vice president had already come to his conclusions and wanted to find data to back up these conclusions. This approach was opposed to how CIA analysts typically worked: by carefully gathering data, verifying it with as many trustworthy sources as possible, and only then drawing conclusions.[22]

Distrustful of the CIA and not satisfied with what they were giving him about Iraq, Cheney's office demanded to be given raw, unconfirmed information from the agency. Specifically, Cheney's assistant for national security affairs, Scooter Libby, demanded such data from the CIA, believing he and others could comb them for nuggets of damning information the agency had missed or was somehow unwilling to take seriously. Cheney's office used these unverified data, along with other questionable sources, to insist the Iraqis had tried to purchase "yellowcake" uranium from the African country of Niger, with which they could make nuclear weapons. As it turned out, this story was based on documents that had been forged in Italy by an individual who wanted to make a huge amount of money by selling alleged intelligence.[23]

Cheney's office also charged that the Iraqis were purchasing aluminum tubes for use in nuclear centrifuges, even though scientists from the US Department of Energy concluded the tubes were much too small for use in a nuclear centrifuge and were actually being acquired to construct conventional rocket launchers.

Then there was the bogus claim that Iraq was using mobile weapons labs that could escape easy detection by weapons inspectors. This allegation was based on German intelligence agents' interviews with an Iraqi defector known only as "Curveball." The CIA never interviewed him, and what they did learn from the Germans did not make any logical sense. The Germans themselves suspected Curveball was giving them this information because he wanted to obtain resettlement aid from their government. In the end, the German operatives themselves concluded Curveball was unreliable and conveyed this view to the CIA.

Then there were assertions of direct links between al-Qaeda and Iraq. One such claim held there had been a meeting between Mohamed Atta, one of the 9/11 hijackers, and an Iraq intelligence agent in Prague. There were no eyewitness reports or recordings of the supposed meeting, and the CIA failed to find any other evidence it had taken place. According to the FBI, Atta was in Florida and then in Virginia at the time the rendezvous was supposed to have occurred, findings that were confirmed in 2004 by the independent, bipartisan 9/11 Commission.[24] And none other than Dick Cheney admitted during an interview on NBC's *Meet the Press* in September

2006 that neither the CIA nor the FBI had been able to confirm the Prague connection had taken place.[25] Reason alone should have led Cheney and his office long before to conclude that Hussein and the Iraqis had nothing to gain from any cooperation with al-Qaeda or any other Islamic terrorist groups. Hussein and his regime were members of the secular Baath Party, the greatest threat to which were Islamic militants such as al-Qaeda.[26]

Another claim held that Iraqis had provided training with chemical and biological weapons to al-Qaeda members. This story came from Ibn al-Shaykh al-Libi, a Libyan national who had been captured in Afghanistan. The CIA sent him to Egypt for "enhanced interrogation," where, under torture, he told about this supposed link between Iraq and al-Qaeda. He later recanted these allegations after being confronted with evidence from other CIA detainees who contradicted his claims.[27]

Clearly, none of this seemingly damning evidence was true. The Iraqis had not tried to purchase yellowcake uranium; the aluminum tubes had been acquired to house conventional rockets; there were no mobile labs; and the Iraqis had not trained al-Qaeda operatives in the use of chemical and biological weapons. Yet the administration would not let go of these stories. And in trying to blame Iraq for 9/11, the administration was playing on public credulity. Why would the United States be preparing to go to war in Iraq, many people asked themselves, unless Iraq were responsible in a large way for the 9/11 attacks on the United States? In addition, it was hard for most people to believe such attacks would be possible without state support. Indeed, the Bush administration itself never did adjust to the idea that terrorism was a problem that was, more often than not, a stateless phenomenon—or that it could be used as a weapon to destabilize states from the inside.

President Bush did not directly blame Iraq for the 9/11 attacks, but he and various members of his administration continued to drop strong hints to this effect, which caused many Americans to believe the Iraqis were culpable. For instance, in his 2003 State of the Union address, Bush said, "Imagine those nineteen hijackers with other weapons and other plans—this time armed by Saddam Hussein. It would take one vial, one canister, one crate slipped into this country to bring a day of horror like none we have ever known."[28] On March 16 of that year, Cheney appeared on *Meet the Press* and declared Hussein had had "a long-standing relationship with al-Qaeda."[29] This assertion was untrue, but the American people had no way of knowing this at the time.

Statements by other members of the administration also convinced many in the public that a war against Iraq was both necessary and justified. These included pronouncements by Condoleezza Rice, who was Bush's national security advisor from 2001 to 2005 and secretary of state from 2005 to 2009. Although not a neocon herself, Rice supported "transformational diplomacy," which would engender democracy in Middle Eastern countries. On CNN, she declared there was "increasing evidence that [Hussein] continues his march toward weapons of mass destruction." The only evidence she cited were the aluminum tubes, which she insisted were "only really suited for nuclear weapons programs."[30] It is unclear if she believed this claim at the time, but, in fact, it was false. On September 25, 2002, she proclaimed on the *PBS NewsHour* that the Iraqi dictator was providing "training to al-Qaeda in chemical weapons development."[31] This assertion was unproven at the time and also turned out to be untrue. On January 10, 2003, Rice did an interview with CNN's Wolf Blitzer and said, "The problem here is that there will always be some uncertainty about how quickly he [Hussein] can acquire nuclear weapons. But we don't want the smoking gun to be a mushroom cloud."[32]

Meanwhile, Secretary of State Colin Powell remained dubious. Powell was one of the most admired and respected people in American public life and was not a neocon. He had served as chairman of the Joint Chiefs of Staff during the Persian Gulf War, was a retired four-star general, and the first African American secretary of state. So what he had to say to the president should have carried much weight.

During dinner with Bush on August 5, 2002, as Powell recalled in his autobiography, "I wanted to make sure [the president] understood that military action and its aftermath had serious consequences, many of which would be unforeseen, dangerous, and hard to control." Powell also remembered that most of the discussions about invading Iraq had focused on military operations and on getting rid of Saddam Hussein, while "not enough attention had been given either to non-military options or the aftermath of a military conquest." But contrary to the administration's war plans, Powell wrote, "Wars break things, kill people, and leave in their wake horrendous confusion, chaos, and physical and social upheavals." Most especially, "religious, political, or ethnic rivalries, kept under a lid before the invasion, may erupt unpredictably in the invasion's aftermath." And it was extremely naïve to assume that Iraq could "somehow transform itself into a stable country with democratic leaders ninety days after we took Baghdad." Powell believed that "such hopes were unrealistic," and he "was sure that we would be in for a longer struggle."[33]

Powell's pithy summary for warning the president merits quoting in full:

> I had come up with a simple expression that summarized these ideas for the President: "If you break it, you own it." It was shorthand for the profound reality that if we take out another country's government by force, we instantly become the new government, responsible for governing the country and for the security of its people until we can turn all that over to a new, stable, and functioning government. We are now in charge. We have to be prepared to take charge.[34]

President Bush should have heeded Powell's very prescient warnings and not have ordered an invasion of Iraq. The United States—and the Iraqi people, in particular—would have been spared untold misery that went on for years and years, as chaos, civil war, religious and sectarian strife, and new waves of terrorism broke out in many corners of the world. In the end, arrogance, willful ignorance, and stoking fear among the public won the day.

Ten days after Powell's dinner with the president, on August 15, a devastating op-ed piece appeared in the *Wall Street Journal*. Its author was Brent Scowcroft, who had served as Bush 41's national security advisor. Under the headline "Don't Attack Iraq," Scowcroft wrote that an Iraq War might well prove a distraction from the larger war on terrorism. It would not be the "cakewalk," he added, that some in the administration were predicting. The consequences would be costly in blood and treasure and "could well destabilize Arab regimes in the region" and require "a large-scale, long-term military occupation."[35] The president was furious and called his father to ask if Scowcroft had told him about the forthcoming op-ed. The senior Bush affirmed that Scowcroft had told him about the article, but he added that he had not tried to dissuade him. Bush 41's biographer, Jon Meacham, does not believe that the former president intentionally used Scowcroft to relay a message to his son. Still, Bush 41 assured Bush 43, "Brent's a good man. He's a friend—Brent's your friend," a none too veiled way of saying Scowcroft's opinions should be weighed in the deliberations over going to war. Of course, Bush feared that many would suppose his father had used Scowcroft as a messenger— as many readers of the op-ed piece did, in fact, conclude.[36]

As Bush 43 remembered it in an interview with Meacham, his father had made no direct, personal recommendations about the decision to go to war—or, later, about the prosecution of the war. Communications between him and his father fell into two categories, he recalled: "Half the time he'd be telling me, 'Son, you're doing fine,' . . . and half the time he'd be railing about what somebody had said about me." Bush added he seldom sought his father's advice on any major issue, explaining, "He and I both understood that I had access to more and better information than he did."[37] But in what seems like an especially depreciatory comment about his father, Bush told journalist Bob Woodward during an interview that the senior Bush was "the wrong father to appeal to in terms of strength. There is a higher father that I appeal to."[38] Both the Bushes later told Meacham that the comment was "more theological than Freudian"—that it was about the son's religious faith and reliance on God in times of crisis.[39]

Yet the senior Bush's comments about Vice President Dick Cheney suggest he did have some serious qualms about his son's Iraq policy. He told Meacham he was puzzled over how Cheney seemed to be a "changed man" from the person who had served earlier as his secretary of defense. When Meacham asked when the first President Bush began to think Cheney had changed, he responded, "The reaction to [the attacks of 9/11], what to do about the Middle East. . . . Just iron-ass. His seeming knuckling under the real hard-charging guys who want to fight about everything, use force to get our way in the Middle East."[40] He also believed that, as vice president, Cheney should have been more discreet in his opinions by conveying them to the president alone, as he himself had done as Reagan's vice president. Instead, Cheney and his "hard-charging" staff promoted their view in policy meetings at the White House, elsewhere in the government, and in the media. In addition, Bush 41 believed his son had made a big mistake in "letting Cheney bring in kind of his own State Department," which gave the hawkish vice president and the neocons undue influence on the administration. In the end, though, his son was responsible for what was done in Iraq. "The buck stops there," the senior Bush said to Meacham.[41]

It is unfortunate Bush 41 did not share his qualms about going to war in Iraq directly to his son. It is equally unfortunate his son did not heed the warnings of Scowcroft and Powell about attacking Iraq.

Equally disturbing was the administration's disregard of expert opinion from its own State Department. In contrast to lead-ups to war in the Philippines and in Vietnam, when experts on these places were few or nonexistent, the State Department in 2002 and 2003 had abundant knowledge about Iraq and the likely outcomes from a war there. However, Bush and his advisors chose to ignore these expert insights. For instance, Under Secretary of State Paula Dobriansky, along with three senior members of the State Department, warned in a memo that "a failure to address short-term public security and humanitarian assistance concerns could result in serious human rights abuses which would undermine an otherwise successful military campaign, and our reputation internationally."[42] Such comments, combined with Secretary Powell's warnings to Bush in person, should have given the president great pause.

During the past months, the Republicans had been using the lead-up to war, along with fears of possible new terrorist threats, to elect Republicans to the House and Senate in the off-year elections of 2002. Republican candidates repeated over and over that President Bush and their party had kept the country safe in the aftermath of 9/11. When the votes were in, the Republicans picked up two seats in the Senate, giving them a slim majority, and added to their majority in the House by eight members. For the first time since 1934, in the midst of Roosevelt's New Deal, the president's party had added seats in an off-year election. War—in this case, threats of war—had helped the Republicans politically.

Meanwhile, the administration continued to make dubious assertions to Congress as part of a campaign to convince it to authorize the use of force against Iraq. In response to incessant claims by the president and those around him that Hussein was making and stockpiling weapons of mass destruction, the Senate Intelligence Committee asked the CIA to prepare a National Intelligence Estimate. The agency had to rush to put the estimate together in just three weeks. The resulting ninety-five-page document, delivered to Capitol Hill on October 1, 2002, repeated all the familiar charges that had been made against Iraq and the rationale for them, but it also contained many caveats and dissents, especially in the appendices. Unfortunately, when the document was made available to members of the House and Senate, the vast majority of them did not bother to read it. Neither, by their own admissions, did President Bush and Condoleezza Rice.[43] The administration was clearly determined to go to war, regardless of the evidence.

Although Democrats in particular were dubious about the president's request to authorize force, they did not want to be accused of being soft on either Iraq or terrorism—like accusations of being soft on Communism during the Cold War. The war authorization vote came on October 16, 2002. The House passed the resolution 293–133; the Senate, 77–23. The resolution gave Bush the power to use military force "as he determines to be necessary and appropriate to defend the national security of the United States against the continuing threat posed by Iraq," as well as to enforce all relevant UN Security Council resolutions relating to Iraq. Some skeptical members of both houses comforted themselves by concluding they had only voted to authorize war as a last resort. They may have also been comforted by the president's prediction—wildly incorrect, as it turned out—that the war would be over in six months.

Not only was Congress remiss in not questioning what the administration was telling them, but the news media also failed to offer any substantial criticism during the run-up to war. Like members of Congress, media CEOs, along with their reporters and news analysts, did not want to be accused of lacking patriotism—or of, in effect, calling the president a liar. In addition, news outlets had long realized war scares were good for circulation and sales. Some news outlets even fired reporters who came up with stories that contradicted the government line. After the war in Iraq did begin, the media agreed to have their reporters embedded with US military units. The media also refrained from showing dead and mangled bodies during the early stages of the conflict, and the Department of Defense did not allow television outlets to show flag-draped coffins of fallen soldiers being delivered home.[44]

Even the august *New York Times* bought the official story line. For example, *Times* reporter Judith Miller wrote a story in September 2002, sourced by the administration itself, claiming Iraq was buying aluminum tubes for its nuclear centrifuges. When Miller was informed most scientists doubted the story, she and a fellow reporter admitted that there had been some debate among intelligence experts but that it was nevertheless "the intelligence agencies' unanimous view that the types of tubes that Iraq has been seeking are used to make such centrifuges."[45] Cheney and Rice then went on the Sunday talk shows and cited the article as proof of the aluminum tubes story, as if the *Times* article were an independent source—which it most assuredly was not, since it had been fed to the reporter by the administration. In a series of articles that followed, Miller continued to put forth the administration's line about WMD without questioning it in any way. Later, after no WMD were found, the *Times* editors apologized, saying, "We wish we had been more aggressive in re-examining the claims as new evidence emerged—or failed to emerge."[46] By then, the damage had been done. Such unquestioning stories in the prestigious *New York Times* and in other mainstream media, including radio and television, helped to convince 69 percent of the public that Saddam Hussein had been personally involved in the attacks on 9/11 and 57 percent that Iraq was a key supporter of al-Qaeda. As late as 2008, 48 percent of the public believed Hussein had played a large role in the attacks.

Bush and Cheney had originally opposed going through the United Nations to support American policies, but Powell insisted the United States needed the organization's backing and approval. British prime minister Tony Blair also wanted authorization from the

United Nations as cover for his support of the United States in the face of tremendous British opposition to participating in an Iraq war.

In November 2002, the United States convinced the UN Security Council to vote unanimously that Iraq was in "material breach" of earlier resolutions concerning weapons of mass destruction. It declared Baghdad must allow enhanced weapons inspections or face "serious consequences." A team of UN inspectors led by Hans Blix entered Iraq late that month to begin operations. At the same time, Defense Secretary Rumsfeld began moving military units into the Persian Gulf area.

On December 7, the Iraqis submitted a long document to the United Nations, as required by the resolution, stating they had no unconventional weapons stockpiles and no program for building nuclear weapons. The Bush administration insisted the Iraqis were lying because they did not admit to trying to purchase yellowcake uranium from Niger and buying aluminum tubes for use in a nuclear centrifuge, even though the CIA had already dismissed the Niger story and scientists from the US Department of Energy had concluded the tubes were unsuitable for that use. What is more, over the next few months, the UN inspectors found nothing on the ground in Iraq in the way of weapons violations.

Secretary Powell continued to hope for a peaceful resolution in Iraq. In order to avoid a second war with Iraq, Powell wanted to keep the inspections going for as long as possible while building up American forces and to pressure the United Nations to threaten military force if Hussein did not come clean. These actions, Powell thought, might lead to an internal coup against the Iraqi dictator.

Whatever his misgivings, Powell was a good soldier, and he had promised President Bush he would support his policies toward Iraq. However, Powell did not want to go before the UN Security Council and ask for a declaration to use military force unless he had an "airtight" argument to make against Iraq. Scooter Libby wrote a draft of a speech for Powell. After hours of fact-checking, Powell's team at the State Department concluded Libby had "cherry-picked" anything and everything that might make a case. They tossed out the Libby document and began working on their own draft based on the National Intelligence Estimate that had been submitted to Congress, but even many of that document's assertions were thought unsubstantiated or questionable.

Although Powell himself rejected many of the claims in the National Intelligence Estimate, he went ahead with his speech to the UN Security Council, delivered February 5, 2003. Despite doubts, he had pledged to support the president's drive to war, and he was not about to let down the commander in chief, to whom he had given his word.

Many of his assertions were already in doubt or would soon be proven incorrect. He insisted the Iraqis had not accounted for all the WMD they had possessed a dozen years before at the end of the Persian Gulf War, and he added, "We know . . . of the existence of mobile production facilities used to make biological agents."[47] Powell mentioned the aluminum tubes but took care to state that, although some doubts about their purpose had surfaced, most experts believed they were for use in nuclear centrifuges. (In fact, most experts did not believe this.) He went on to insist there was a sinister network between Iraq and al-Qaeda terrorists, even though the CIA had recently discounted such a network (a fact Powell may not have known at the time of the speech). In any case, Powell's presentation was not enough to persuade either France or Russia, which, as permanent members of the Security Council, held a veto over its decisions. Both announced on March 17 that they would not support the resolution to use force against Iraq.

Powell later believed that this speech to the United Nations became the most important public case for going to war against Iraq and that it convinced many in Congress the case was sound. He also came to realize very soon that much of the information given to him to make his argument was wrong. In his autobiography, he wrote, "I've asked myself again and again: 'Should I have seen the National Intelligence Estimate's weaknesses? Should I have sniffed them out? Did my critical instincts fail me?'" He was especially angered when he began reading books and articles by former CIA officials who expressed amazement over what they saw as "unsupported claims" in his UN speech. But Powell refused to place the blame on others, writing, "A blot, a failure, will always be attached to me and my UN presentation. But I am mad mostly at myself for not having smelled the problem. My instincts failed me."[48] Conspicuously, no one else in the administration bearing responsibility for the war has come even close to making such a confession.

Despite the fact the UN inspectors had not found any WMD in Iraq, despite the fact the yellowcake uranium and aluminum tube assertions were false, and despite the fact allegations of ties between Hussein and al-Qaeda terrorists were groundless, President Bush was determined to have his war against Iraq. Such facts simply did not seem to matter to the president, who now switched to emphasizing the benefits of implanting democracy in Iraq and of having it spread from there throughout the region—the reverse domino theory. At the end of February 2003, he spoke before the American Enterprise Institute in Washington, where he told the crowd of 1,500 people, "The world has a clear interest in the spread of democratic values. . . . A new regime in Iraq would serve as a dramatic and inspiring example of freedom for other nations in the region."[49]

In effect, Bush was going to war no matter what. This attitude caused House Majority Leader Dick Armey, a Republican, to declare Bush and administration officials were in the grip of a "he-man macho psychosis where they felt the need to go out and shoot somebody to show they're the tough guy on the block."[50]

Bush biographer Jean Edward Smith believes the president's evangelical religious beliefs also helped to stiffen his resolve and allow him to ignore advice about attacking Iraq. In 1985, he had undergone a religious conversion, which he later credited with giving him the strength and resolve to overcome his alcoholism. In the aftermath of 9/11, he believed going to war was a divinely appointed mission: "This is what I was put on earth for. I'm here for a reason."[51] During a telephone conversation with French president Jacques Chirac, in an effort to persuade Chirac to have his country vote in the United Nations to authorize the use of force Bush referred to a story from the apocalyptic biblical book of Revelation. "Gog and Magog," he told Chirac, "are at work in the Middle East. Biblical prophecies are being fulfilled. This confrontation is willed by God, who wants us to use this conflict to erase His people's enemies before a new age begins."[52]

A dumbfounded Chirac had no idea what Bush was talking

about—that Gog and Magog were images from Revelation that evangelicals used to personify the last great battle that would signal the return of Christ. Almost exactly a century earlier, President McKinley had convinced himself, in a much gentler way, that God wanted him to use force to conquer the Philippines—with disastrous results.

Of course, Bush did not publicly claim God had ordained him to invade Iraq. Rather, the decision to go to war was stated in more secular terms and flowed from various foreign policy statements and principles that, taken together, have been called the "Bush Doctrine." In his 2010 memoir, *Decision Points*, Bush listed briefly the main points of the doctrine:

1. Make no distinction between terrorists and the nations that harbor them—and hold both to account [with the assumption that terrorists are sheltered and enabled by states].
2. Take the fight to the enemy overseas before they can attack us again here at home [the doctrine of preemption].
3. Confront threats before they fully materialize [an extension of preemption].
4. Advance liberty and hope as an alternative to the enemy's ideology of repression and fear [the reverse domino theory].[53]

Although Bush used the doctrine of preemption in the second point to justify war against Iraq, he was really calling for a preventative war. A preemptive conflict is one that seeks to obtain a strategic advantage in an imminent and unavoidable war. A preventative war, on the other hand, is one undertaken to keep another power from acquiring the ability to attack—that is, a war intended to take out a potential threat when an attack is not imminent or even known to be in the planning. Clearly, the administration had no evidence Iraq was planning to attack the United States or any other power, meaning that the president was actually launching a preventative war, not a preemptive war. And preventative wars, without the approval of the United Nations, are considered illegal in international law. Since the Security Council had failed to authorize Bush's preventative war, one could argue that it was, in fact, an illegal war.[54]

As it became clear the United States was going to war against

Iraq, massive demonstrations occurred in hundreds of cities around the world. On February 15 alone, estimates are that ten to fifteen million people took to the streets to protest, including some three million in Rome and more than one million in London. About two hundred thousand demonstrated against the war in New York and San Francisco. Millions more marched in the weeks that followed.[55]

Ignoring all warnings and even common sense, as well as the massive demonstrations and the fact Iraq posed no current threat to the United States, Bush finally got his war. It was neither necessary nor a last resort, and it was arguably illegal. Nevertheless, in a televised address from the White House on March 17, 2003, the president gave Saddam Hussein an ultimatum: he and his sons would have to leave Iraq within forty-eight hours or there would be war. Despite not receiving the imprimatur of the United Nations, he had managed to persuade several countries—most important, the United Kingdom—to join in an invasion of Iraq.

A British government inquiry, headed by Sir John Chilcot, which was published in July 2016, amounted to a devastating criticism of the decision by Prime Minister Tony Blair to support the march to war. Known officially as the Iraq Inquiry, the massive report of 2.6 million words leveled several charges: The Blair government had used flawed intelligence to make its case and had failed to exhaust all diplomatic possibilities. In addition, Iraq had not been an immediate threat to British national security, and the government had made no plans for what should be done once Saddam Hussein was removed from power. As such, the Iraq Inquiry has reinforced American criticism of the Bush administration's similar and false justifications for attacking Iraq.[56]

The actual operation began on March 20, 2003. At first, the war went well, as Iraqi forces collapsed and then melted away. Very soon, however, widespread looting broke out, US and allied forces were attacked by a variety of armed groups in Iraq, and a full-scale civil war gripped the land. By 2014, it looked as if the country were disintegrating amid sectarian fighting. Democracy did not triumph in Iraq, and there was no spread of democracy throughout the region. Approximately 4,400 Americans lost their lives, and 32,000 were seriously wounded. Some estimates put the number of Iraqi dead from both direct and indirect causes, most of them civilians, at close to

250,000. The conflict would cost the American people between $4 trillion and $7 trillion, if one figures in interest payments on the money borrowed to pay for fighting, as well as the funds that will be required over the next several decades to cover veterans' health care and other benefits.[57]

Ignoring the warnings of Colin Powell and others in the State Department, Secretary Rumsfeld and his Department of Defense had done little planning for the aftermath of war, simply assuming the Americans would be greeted as liberators and democracy would break out spontaneously. When Rumsfeld was asked at a press conference in April 2003 about the looting early in the war, he simply said with a grin, "Stuff happens."[58] Nor were he and others in the administration contrite when months of searching for WMD by US military teams failed to turn up anything. Instead, when asked in November 2003 why he had insisted earlier that he knew where the WMD were located, Rumsfeld said flippantly, "Sometimes I overstate for emphasis."[59] Nor were members of the administration apologetic about the damage the war had done to world public opinion about the United States, which was now widely regarded as an arrogant bully. The administration had squandered not only the nation's moral authority but also the worldwide sympathy and goodwill for the United States in the aftermath of the 9/11 terror attacks. Typical at that time had been the headline in France's *Le Monde*, "*Nous sommes tous Americains*" ("We are all Americans").[60]

During the presidential election of 2004, the Republicans played on fears of another 9/11 if Democratic candidate John Kerry were elected. In a campaign speech, Vice President Cheney insisted, "It's absolutely essential that eight weeks from today . . . we make the right choice. Because if we make the wrong choice, then the danger is that we'll get hit again, that we'll be hit in a way that will be devastating."[61] At that point, the American death toll in Iraq had just reached one thousand, which is another reason the Republicans chose to warn the public that another 9/11 was likely to occur if Kerry were elected. The strategy apparently paid off: Bush was reelected with sixty-two million to Kerry's fifty-nine million popular votes. The count in the Electoral College was 286–251. According to the exit polls, Bush did extremely well among those who named terrorism as one of their top concerns. The Republicans gained three seats in the House of Representatives and four seats in the Senate, allowing them to maintain control of both chambers. By being elected to a second term, Bush achieved something that had eluded his father, and he could claim this time to have a genuine mandate from the American people.

Flush from his victory at the polls, the president decided he would make his inaugural address a "freedom speech." The United States had failed to find any WMD in Iraq, so now Bush fell back on the proposition that the country was delivering democracy to Iraq, as well as to oppressed peoples all over the world. In this second inaugural address, Bush equated American security with the spread of democracy: "We have seen our vulnerability and we have seen its deepest source. . . . As long as whole regions of the world simmer in resistance and tyranny . . . violence will gather and multiply in destructive power." The only force that could break this vicious cycle, according to Bush, was "human freedom." As a result, it was the "policy of the United States to seek and support the growth of democratic movements and institutions in every nation and culture, with the ultimate goal of ending tyranny in our world." Tellingly, given his country's recent and now failing attempts to introduce democracy by force of arms in Iraq, the president declared bringing about democracy was "not primarily the task of arms"; nor, he added, would it happen quickly. If oppressed people stood for liberty, he promised, "We will stand with you."[62] Just what this meant was unclear, but it seemed Bush, without specifically admitting it, was backing away from the only remaining justification for war in Iraq and returning, perhaps, to the spirit of what he had recommended for American foreign policy during his 2000 campaign. Then, he had said:

> I just don't think it's the role of the United States to walk into a country and say, we do it this way, so should you. I think the United States must be humble and must be proud and confident of our values, but humble in how we treat nations that are figuring out how to chart their own course.[63]

The news from Iraq continued to be grim. Each evening, there were reports of bombings, assassinations, sectarian conflict, ethnic cleansing, and political stalemate, with Iraq no closer to becoming a democracy than ever. It was more and more difficult for Bush to maintain an upbeat mood. In the words of biographer Peter Baker, "For the first time, he worried he would not succeed in Iraq, that he had gotten himself and the country enmeshed in another Vietnam—again with devastating consequences."[64] At the same time, he and the administration were so consumed with the war that the domestic agenda for the second term was going nowhere. As with Lyndon Johnson, an ill-conceived and increasingly unpopular war was wrecking Bush's presidency.

By the end of 2006, many in Congress, including a number of key Republicans; many media voices; and even some generals thought it was time to bring the troops home. Republican senator Chuck Hagel and Democratic senator Harry Reid both compared the situation in Iraq to Vietnam. In May 2007, the House and Senate approved a bill that required the troops to be withdrawn by March 2008. Bush vetoed it. As the president was about to give his State of the Union address in 2007, only 33 percent of Americans approved of his job performance,

Regardless of the mounting opposition and unpopularity, Bush was not about to admit that the Iraq War had been based on false arguments, that it had been unnecessary as well as disastrous. To say so would mean thousands of American troops and hundreds of thousands of Iraqis had died or been maimed for nothing. Here was proof once again that it is far easier to start a war than to end it, particularly if one winds up on the losing side.

Half a dozen years after Bush left office in 2009, the violent legacies of the war in Iraq continued to plague the Middle East and endanger the security of the United States itself. Foreign policy analysts are in wide agreement that the destabilization of Iraq following the American invasion was the main catalyst for the rise of the Islamic State. This movement has been known by various names as it has evolved over the years since the invasion: the Islamic State of Iraq (ISL), the Islamic State of Iraq and the Levant (ISLE), the Islamic State of Iraq and Syria (ISIS), and simply the Islamic State (IS). Unlike earlier Islamist revolutionary groups that used terror to gain and keep power, the Islamic State decided to seize and control territory. Its espoused goal is to recreate a caliphate, a type of Islamic government headed by a caliph, who claims to be the religious and political successor of the Prophet Muhammad and the leader of all Muslims.

In fact, Abu Musab al-Zarqawi, the man who founded a terrorist cell that went on to become the Islamic State, was thrilled by the American invasion of Iraq in 2003. The invasion, he believed, would touch off a holy war against the infidel West, in which Islam would surely triumph and lead to the establishment of a new caliphate.[65]

If the anarchy and disarray created by the American invasion did not result in a colossal holy war between the West and Islam, it did produce conditions that were ripe for sectarian conflict and religious fanaticism, which the Islamic State went on to exploit. Contributing powerfully to these conditions were disastrous decisions by the Americans soon after the fall of Baghdad. These included the disbanding of the Iraqi military, the dismissal of the Iraqi civil servants, and the outlawing of the ruling Baath Party. All three entities were bulwarks of Iraqi secular nationalism. Although Saddam Hussein headed the Baath Party, he could have been removed from power without disbanding it. And since Sunni Muslims held most of the important positions in the party, as well as in the military and the civil bureaucracy, the American dismantling of all three resulted in strong Sunni opposition to the occupation. This Sunni anger was stoked even further when American authorities brought in rival Shi'a Muslims as replacements in the Iraqi government, military, and police.

Further undermining American credibility and feeding support for radical militias was the shocking abuse of Iraqi prisoners. In what looked like a case of déjà vu, investigative journalist Seymour Hersh, who had revealed the My Lai atrocities in Vietnam thirty-five years earlier, laid out the story of abuses at the American-run Abu Ghraib prison near Baghdad. His account appeared in the *New Yorker* magazine in May 2004, a week after similar revelations on CBS's *60 Minutes*.[66] Both the television program and the magazine article included graphic photographs of torture and humiliation. As in the Philippines and Vietnam, the American tormenters had photographed their own inhuman treatment of individuals under their power.

Hersh relied heavily in his article on a fifty-three-page report by Gen. Antonio M. Taguba of an investigation into the army's prison system in Iraq. It had been completed in February 2004. Although the report was not intended for public release, the *New Yorker* was able to obtain a copy. Taguba reported many instances of "sadistic, blatant, and wanton criminal abuses of prisoners that had taken place at Abu Ghraib between October and December of 2003."[67] In one especially shocking paragraph, Taguba summarized the methods of torture that had been used:

> Breaking chemical lights and pouring the phosphoric liquid on detainees; pouring cold water on naked detainees; beating detainees with a broom handle and a chair; threatening male detainees with rape; allowing a military police guard to stitch the wound of a detainee who was injured after being slammed against the wall in his cell; sodomizing a detainee with a chemical light and perhaps a broom stick, and using military working dogs to frighten and intimidate detainees with threats of attack, and in one instance actually biting a detainee.[68]

Testimony and photographs revealed that prisoners were, in fact, sodomized, forced to masturbate and perform homosexual acts, stripped naked and forced to lie on cold cell floors, deprived of running water or toilet facilities, threatened with electrocution and attacks by vicious dogs, and, in several instances, beaten to death. Prisoners were also subjected to waterboarding, a form of torture similar to the "water cure" American troops had used on Filipinos a century before. Such treatment was justified as "enhanced interrogation," even though intelligence experts had long known using force or humiliation almost always fails, since subjects will invariably tell their inquisitors what they think they want to hear.[69]

Those accused of misconduct at the prison used the old and discredited excuse that they were just following orders. Back home, President Bush insisted their behavior was a rare exception by a few individuals, but the Taguba report shows the mistreatment of prisoners was both routine and widespread. Indeed, Taguba believed the treatment of prisoners at Abu Ghraib violated both army regulations

and the Geneva Conventions.[70] Bush's denial of any systematic violations is very similar to the assertions of presidents during the wars in
Vietnam and the Philippines that any instances of wrongdoing were
mere aberrations.

This time, fortunately, the US Army took the allegations of abuse
seriously, and nine perpetrators were convicted. They received prison
sentences ranging from ten years to six months. All were enlistees,
and no officers were charged, even though it was argued by defense
attorneys that officers had ordered that prisoners "be broken" or had
sent out memos saying such things as "The gloves are coming off
regarding these detainees."[71]

Understandably, Iraqis were enraged after hearing about torture
and mistreatment at Abu Ghraib, and these events provided more
fuel for radical Islamic groups. Among these groups was a collection
of Sunni fighters calling themselves al-Qaeda in Iraq. Despite the
Bush administration's earlier insistence that Saddam Hussein had
had ties to al-Qaeda, the organization did not exist in Iraq until the
American invasion and occupation led to chaos in the country.

Al-Qaeda in Iraq was led by al-Zarqawi, who changed the group's
name in 2006 to the Islamic State of Iraq (ISI). Under this and successive names, the Islamic State engaged in bombings, kidnappings,
and beheadings. In 2011, what was now renamed ISIS and under the
leadership of Abu Bakr al-Baghdadi moved across the border from
Iraq into Syria, where it took advantage of power vacuums spawned
by a civil war in that country. At this point, the Islamic State began to
seize control of territory in both Iraq and Syria as a first step in creating the long-dreamed-of caliphate.[72]

The Islamic State continued to use extreme brutality to hold territory and to intimidate anyone who might oppose it. It also used
these extreme measures to impress potential recruits in both the
Middle East and beyond. In November 2015, Islamic State terrorists living in France and Belgium killed 130 people in Paris. Then,
in December of the same year, an American husband and wife who
had been inspired by the Islamic State, but apparently not under
direct orders from ISIS, killed sixteen people in San Bernardino, California. In March 2016, ISIS claimed responsibility for bombings in
Brussels, Belgium, that killed thirty-two people.

The American invasion of Iraq had opened a seemingly unending string of catastrophes. At the time of this writing, there seemed no end in sight to the fighting in Iraq, to the violence that had spread into neighboring Syria, and to the Islamic State's attacks in countries far beyond the Middle East. In unraveling Iraq, the United States had unleashed a torrent of woes.

CHAPTER 8

THE REVELATIONS
OF HISTORY

"One cannot undo the past, but the assessment of
past errors is absolutely indispensable to efforts to
correct them and to avoiding their repetition."
—Sen. J. William Fulbright

We study the past for a variety of interrelated reasons: to
gain keener insights into the human condition, to discover how we arrived at present circumstances, and to learn lessons
about how to make better decisions in the future. This historical
inquiry into three American wars—in the Philippines, in Vietnam,
and in Iraq—fought roughly over a century embraces all three historical approaches. But it is mainly offered as a series of cautionary
tales that hopefully can inform decisions about war and peace in the
years ahead.

It is obvious the specific reasons for fighting each of these three
wars were different, as were the persons who decided the country
should go to war, the military commanders at home and on battle-
fields, and the types of weapons used. But none of these wars rose to
the level of a "supreme emergency" necessary to protect the life or
vital interests of the nation. On the contrary, these conflicts under-
mined national well-being: the American conquest of the Philippines
made the United States vulnerable to armed attack by Japan, the war
in Vietnam heightened Cold War tensions that threatened to spill
over into nuclear conflict, and the Iraq War exacerbated terrorist
threats and terrorist actions against the United States and its allies.

And all three conflicts contradicted basic American values, especially the right of self-determination for all peoples. Atrocities committed by some American forces in these wars put into question the moral standing of the United States.

Of course, as is often said, "Hindsight is 20/20." Still, it is helpful to review the reasons why the decision makers—and especially various presidents—led the United States into needless wars with disastrous consequences. One reason was ignorance—at times, willing ignorance—of the facts. When it came to war in the Philippines, President McKinley privately admitted his lack of knowledge about the islands and their people. And no one else in the government knew any more at that time. However, arrogance about growing American power at the turn of the twentieth century, combined with assertions of racial superiority, were thought sufficient to overcome any lack of knowledge about the Philippines—or about obstacles that might be confronted in the islands. Then, there was an unreasoning fear that if the United States did not annex the Philippines, they would fall into the hands of commercial rivals, who would then be in a better position to exploit Asian (especially Chinese) markets—even though there was a much better alternative to annexation. That alternative was American recognition of Philippine independence, combined with genuinely benign and sincere efforts to help the Filipinos maintain that independence.

In Vietnam, the same deadly triad continued to distort and control American policy. As Secretary of Defense Robert McNamara, who served in both the Kennedy and Johnson administrations, wrote in his memoirs, there were no government experts on Vietnam to inform them about the history, culture, and likelihood of American success in that unhappy land. This was not a valid excuse, given that successive administrations could have reached out to scholarly expertise both at home and abroad for information and insight. As with the Philippines, arrogance was brought to bear in the absence of knowledge, at a time when the United States was at its post–World War II height of economic and military power. Fear at this juncture centered on Communism and the unrealistic belief that the Communists in Vietnam were simply part of a much wider conspiracy by China and the Soviet Union to dominate the entire world and that the desire for independence and self-determination in Vietnam had nothing to do with the conflict there.

The case of Iraq is in some ways even more troubling. There was abundant expertise in foreign policy circles, including the State Department, about Iraq and the Middle East as a whole. It is just that the George W. Bush administration did not want to accept or make use of that expertise. And their arrogance was unparalleled: the war would last only six months; the Iraqi people would greet the Americans as liberators; the United States could easily implant democracy in Iraq, where it had never before existed; and, from there, democracy would spread to the rest of the Middle East. Fear that Iraqis possessed weapons of mass destruction was used to galvanize public opinion in favor of the invasion, even though there were serious doubts in many government circles, including the CIA, that such weapons existed—doubts that were confirmed by subsequent failures to find any such weapons. The administration also played on legitimate fears of terrorism in the aftermath of the 9/11 attacks but misdirected this fear by falsely linking the attacks with Iraq.

In all three wars, the media failed to inform the American people objectively or to ask hard questions about the dubious reasons given by those advocating war. In the lead-up to the Spanish-American War and the subsequent decision to attack and occupy the Philippines, much of the mainstream press frequently distorted the truth and fanned the flames of war. Regarding Vietnam, the media, which now included radio and television, did not ask many questions until it was clear the war was going badly. This same lack of skepticism prevailed in the media during the lead-up to the Iraq War.

Political partisanship was also a culprit during these three unnecessary conflicts. When President McKinley hesitated to go to war with Spain, he was accused by some in his own Republican Party of unmanly cowardice. Those who criticized the conduct of the war in the Philippines were denounced as traitors who were giving aid and comfort to the enemy. The worst partisan attacks came during the Vietnam years, when presidents were terrified not to oppose the Vietnamese bid for independence, since they would assuredly be accused of being soft on Communism. Although Republicans were most likely to make such charges against Democrats during the Cold War (of which the Vietnam conflict was a part), Republicans also attacked fellow Republicans for weakness on Communism, and Democrats sometimes leveled similar charges against Republicans. During the Iraq War, the George W. Bush administration used the public's legitimate concern about terrorism to go after critics of plans to invade Iraq or to criticize the war once in progress.

The question is what can be done to prevent future needless wars. It will not be easy, especially since each subsequent generation, including those in power, has a tendency to ignore or forget the lessons of the past. When Ho Chi Minh offered the hand of friendship to the United States just after World War II and asked for recognition of Vietnamese independence, it is unlikely anyone in the Truman administration made comparisons to a similar request for friendship and support half a century earlier from Emilio Aguinaldo in the Philippines. After the American disaster in Vietnam, there was widespread public and political opposition to embarking on future unnecessary conflicts—where national security was not genuinely threatened and where the outcome was uncertain. Fortunately, some Americans did remember the Vietnam debacle and launched huge demonstrations against going to war in Iraq, but to no avail because the Bush administration was determined to go to war, no matter what. Those in Congress who had doubts about an Iraqi war could have opposed the Bush administration more vigorously, but they feared political liability for doing so. In the future, elected representatives will need to be more critical when confronted with calls for war, while others will need to refrain from making charges of disloyalty toward those who sincerely doubt the necessity of using military force. Voters must express their opposition to needless wars at election time by turning out of office those who start or support them. At the same time, the media will have to do a much better job of questioning cries for war. Fortunately, the US Constitution guarantees freedom of speech, freedom of the press (and other forms of media), and freedom of assembly, although these freedoms can be limited temporarily in cases of true national emergency.

The widespread belief the Iraq War never should have been undertaken may well prevent the United States from embarking on unnecessary wars in the foreseeable future. The danger will come when memories of that war fade and some future president is tempted to ignore the lessons of history. The stains of the past can never be erased, but a change in how the nation handles itself in the world can do much to cause these stains to fade. I hope this book may help to prevent thousands of needless deaths and to advance a true American exceptionalism.

NOTES

CHAPTER 1: INTRODUCTION

1. Michael Walzer, *Just and Unjust Wars*, 4th ed. (New York: Basic Books, 2007), 251.
2. Ibid., 252–53.
3. Carl von Clausewitz, *On War*, ed. and trans. Michael Howard and Peter Paret (Princeton, NJ: Princeton University Press, 1976), 605. Clausewitz was still working on this treatise when he died in 1831, though the book was largely completed by 1827.

CHAPTER 2: CUBAN PROLOGUE

1. Quoted in Howard Zinn, *A People's History of the United States* (New York: Harper Perennial, 2005 [1980]), 299.
2. For an excellent overview of the United States at the very end of the nineteenth century, see David Traxel, *1898: The Birth of the American Century* (New York: Vintage Books, 1999).
3. See David R. Contosta, *Rebel Giants: The Revolutionary Lives of Abraham Lincoln and Charles Darwin* (Amherst, NY: Prometheus Books, 2008), 284.
4. John W. Burgess, quoted in Zinn, *People's History*, 299.
5. Josiah Strong, *Our Country: Its Possible Future and Its Present Crisis* (New York: Baker & Taylor, 1885), 165.
6. Quoted in Robert R. Mathisen, *Critical Issues in American Religious History: A Reader* (Waco, TX: Baylor University Press, 2006), 506.
7. Oliver Wendell Holmes Jr., "In Our Youth Our Hearts Were Touched by Fire" (speech, Keene, NH, May 30, 1884). This address was delivered for Memorial Day before John Sedgwick Post No. 4, Grand Army of the Republic. On such attitudes among Civil War veterans, see Stewart McConnell, *Glorious Contentment: The Grand Army of the Republic, 1865–1900* (Chapel Hill: University of North Carolina Press, 1992). And on wider

gender issues in the coming of the war, see Kristin L. Hoganson, *Fighting for American Manhood: How Gender Politics Provoked the Spanish-American and Philippine-American Wars* (New Haven, CT: Yale University Press, 1998).

8. On Reed's opposition to war and imperialism, see Evan Thomas, *The War Lovers: Roosevelt, Lodge, Hearst, and the Rush to Empire, 1898* (New York: Little, Brown, 2010), 108–21.

9. See Lewis L. Gould, *The Spanish-American War and President McKinley* (Lawrence: University Press of Kansas, 1982), 19–53; and Edmund Morris, *The Rise of Theodore Roosevelt* (New York: Coward, McCann & Geoghegan, 1979), 560.

10. William McKinley, "First Inaugural Address of William McKinley," March 4, 1897, transcript, Avalon Project, http://avalon.law.yale.edu/19th_century/mckin1.asp.

11. Morris, *Rise of Theodore Roosevelt*, 559.

12. Theodore Roosevelt, "Naval War College Address," June 2, 1897, transcript, in *Almanac of Theodore Roosevelt*, http://www.theodore-roosevelt.com/images/research/speeches/tr1898.pdf.

13. See the excellent analysis of Gerald F. Linderman in *The Mirror of War: American Society and the Spanish-American War* (Ann Arbor: University of Michigan Press, 1974), 148–73.

14. Quoted in T. Harry Williams, *The History of American Wars from 1745 to 1918* (Baton Rouge: Louisiana State University Press, 1981), 318.

15. See Thomas, *War Lovers*, 151–52.

16. Enrique Dupuy de Lôme, letter, *Spanish-American War Centennial*, http://www.spanamwar.com/Delome.htm (page inaccessible as of November 30, 2016).

17. Roosevelt to Benjamin Harrison Diblee, 16 February 1898, in *Letters of Theodore Roosevelt*, 6 vols., ed. Elting E. Morison (Cambridge, MA: Harvard University Press, 1951–54), 1:783–84.

18. These quotations are from Thomas, *War Lovers*, 210–11.

19. Ibid., 213–14.

20. William McKinley, *Speeches and Addresses of William McKinley* (New York: Doubleday & McClure, 1900), 67–68.

21. Morris, *Rise of Theodore Roosevelt*, 603.

22. Roosevelt to Henry Cabot Lodge, 21 September 1897; Roosevelt to William W. Kimball, 19 November 1897, in Morison, *Letters of Theodore Roosevelt*, 1:690, 716–17.

23. Quoted in Hermann Hagedorn, *Leonard Wood: A Biography*, 2 vols. (New York: Harper and Brothers, 1931), 1:141.

24. Roosevelt, quoted in Morris, *Rise of Theodore Roosevelt*, 611.

25. Quoted in Kathleen Dalton, *Theodore Roosevelt: A Strenuous Life* (New York: Vintage Books, 2004), 170.

26. Ibid., 171.

27. James Boyle, quoted in the *New York Times*, September 1, 1912.

28. H. H. Kohlsaat, *From McKinley to Harding: Personal Recollections of Our Presidents* (New York: Charles Scribner's Sons, 1923), 67.

29. William McKinley, "Message to Congress Requesting a Declaration of War with Spain," April 11, 1898, American Presidency Project, http://www.presidency.ucsb.edu/ws/index.php?pid=103901&st=&st1=.

30. William McKinley, letter to Congress, 25 April 1899, *Spanish-American War Centennial*, http://www.spanamwar.com/McKinleywardec.htm.

31. Linderman, *The Mirror of War*, 119–27; Ruth Miller Elson, *American Schoolbooks in the Nineteenth Century* (Lincoln: University of Nebraska Press, 1964).

32. Quoted in Margaret Leech, *In the Days of McKinley* (New York: Harper and Brothers, 1959), 138, 162.

33. Dalton, *Theodore Roosevelt*, 171.

34. Winthrop Chanler to Margaret Chanler, April 29, 1898, quoted in Morris, *Rise of Theodore Roosevelt*, 612.

35. John Milton Cooper Jr., *The Warrior and the Priest: Woodrow Wilson and Theodore Roosevelt* (Cambridge, MA: Harvard University Press, 1983), 7.

36. Henry Wadsworth Longfellow, "The Musician's Tale; The Saga of King Olaf," Maine Historical Society, http://www.hwlongfellow.org/poems_poem.php?pid=2042.

37. "Adventure 1," *Saga of the Nibelung*, The Viking's World, http://thevikingsworld.com/Skald/nibelungenlied/nibelungenlied001.html.

38. Theodore Roosevelt, *Autobiography* (New York: Macmillan, 1913), 275.

39. Quoted in Morris, *Rise of Theodore Roosevelt*, 636.

40. Ibid., 654.

41. Ibid., 656.

42. William Howard Taft to Edwin P. Parker, November 16, 1914, as quoted in Cooper, *Warrior and the Priest*, 284.

43. Thomas Osbert Mordaunt, "The Call," http://www.wikisource.org/wiki/The_Call_Mordaunt (page inaccessible as of November 30, 2016.

44. Quoted in Morris, *Rise of Theodore Roosevelt*, 661.

45. Ibid., 650.

46. See Linderman, *Mirror of War*, 128–44.

47. Quoted in Dalton, *Theodore Roosevelt,* 173.

48. Ibid.

49. John Hay, quoted in John Taliafero, *All the Great Prizes: The Life of John Hay from Lincoln to Roosevelt* (New York: Simon and Schuster, 2013), 330.

CHAPTER 3: CONQUERING THE PHILIPPINES

1. Quoted in T. Harry Williams, *The History of American Wars from 1745 to 1918* (Baton Rouge: Louisiana State University Press, 1981), 331.

2. Quoted in Gregg Jones, *Honor in the Dust: Theodore Roosevelt, War in the Philippines, and the Rise and Fall of America's Imperial Dream* (New York: New American Library, 2012), 87.

3. Brian McAllister Linn, *The Philippine War, 1899–1902* (Lawrence: University Press of Kansas, 2000), 19.

4. Emilio Aguinaldo, diary entry, in Emilio Aguinaldo and Vicente Albano Pacis, *A Second Look at America* (New York: Robert Spiller and Sons, 1957), 34.

5. George Dewey, *Autobiography* (New York: Charles Scribner's Sons, 1916), 247.

6. Emilio Aguinaldo, quoted in Marcel P. Lichauco and Moorefield Storey, *The Conquest of the Philippines by the United States, 1898–1925* (New York: G. P. Putnam's Sons, 1926), 46.

7. Quoted in ibid., 47.

8. Daniel Schirmer, "How the Philippine-US War Began," *Monthly Review* 51 (September 1999): 46.

9. Quoted in H. W. Brands, *Bound to Empire: The United States and the Philippines* (New York: Oxford University Press, 1992), 49.

10. Jones, *Honor in the Dust,* 103.

11. Whitelaw Reid, *Making Peace with Spain: The Diary of Whitelaw Reid, September–December 1898,* ed. H. Wayne Morgan (Austin: University of Texas Press, 1965), 82.

12. Paul A. Kramer, "Race-Making and Colonial Violence in the US Empire: The Philippine-American War as Race War," *Diplomatic History* 30 (April 2006): 176.

13. James F. Rusling, "Interview with President McKinley," *Christian Advocate,* January 22, 1903.

14. Lewis L. Gould, *The Presidency of William McKinley* (Lawrence: University Press of Kansas, 1980), 141.

15. George Kennan, *American Diplomacy, 1900–1950*, 60th anniversary ed. (Chicago: University of Chicago Press, 2012), 18.

16. Richard Leopold, *Growth of American Foreign Policy* (New York: Knopf, 1962), 212.

17. William McKinley, quoted in the *New York Times*, October 14, 1898.

18. Quoted in Margaret Leech, *In the Days of McKinley* (New York: Harper and Brothers, 1959), 341.

19. Albert J. Beveridge, "March of the Flag" (address to the Indiana Republican Meeting, Indianapolis, IN, September 16, 1898), http://nationalhumanitiescenter.org/pds/gilded/empire/text5/beveridge.pdf.

20. Ibid.

21. William McKinley, "The Benevolent Assimilation" (proclamation, December 21, 1898), http://www.msc.edu.ph/centennial/benevolent.html.

22. Quoted in Lichauco and Storey, *Conquest of the Philippines*, 92.

23. Quoted in ibid., 120.

24. Quoted in Leech, *Days of McKinley*, 358.

25. Schirmer, "How the Philippine-US War," 46–48.

26. Brands, *Bound to Empire*, 49.

27. Rudyard Kipling, "The White Man's Burden: The United States and the Philippine Islands," *McClure's* 12 (February 1899): 290.

28. Jones, *Honor in the Dust*, 143.

29. *Wisconsin Weekly Advocate*, May 17, 1900, as quoted in Kramer, "Race-Making and Colonial Violence," 174.

30. Quoted in Kramer, "Race-Making and Colonial Violence," 189.

31. Quoted in Daniel B. Schirmer, *Republic or Resistance: American Resistance to the Philippine War* (Rochester, VT: Schenkman Books, 1972), 240.

32. Quoted in Kramer, "Race-Making and Colonial Violence," 194.

33. Kramer, "Race-Making and Colonial Violence," 193–94.

34. Ibid., 172.

35. House Document no. 2, *Report of General MacArthur for 1900*, 56th Cong., 2nd Sess. (Washington, DC: US Government Printing Office, 1900), 62.

36. Quoted in Schirmer, *Republic or Resistance*, 225.

37. Senate Document no. 167, *Letter from the Secretary of War*, 56th Cong., 2nd Sess. (Washington, DC: US Government Printing Office, 1900).

38. Orders of J. F. Bell, December 26, 1901, in Moorfield Storey and Julian Codman, eds., *Secretary Root's Record: Marked Severities in Philippine Warfare* (Boston: George H. Ellis, 1902), 73. See also Lichauco and Storey,

Conquest of the Philippines, 120; and Timothy D. Russell, "'I Feel Sorry for These People': African American Soldiers in the Philippine-American War, 1899–1902," *Journal of African American History* 99 (June 2014): 204.

39. Orders of J. F. Bell, December 9, 1901, in Storey and Codman, *Secretary Root's Record*, 68.

40. Clowe's letter appeared in the *Portland Oregonian*, January 29, 1902, and is quoted in Henry Moore Teller, *The Problem in the Philippines* (Whitefish, MT: Kessinger, 1902 [2008]), 58. Teller was a US Senator from Colorado who is best known for sponsoring the Teller Amendment, which forswore American intention of annexing Cuba and was attached to the declaration of war against Spain in 1898.

41. Charles S. Riley's letter home, November 25, 1900, in Storey and Codman, *Secretary Root's Record*, 48.

42. Roosevelt to Herman Speck von Sternberg, 19 July 1902, in *Letters of Theodore Roosevelt*, 6 vols., ed. Elting E. Morison (Cambridge, MA: Harvard University Press, 1951–1954), 3:297–98.

43. For very vivid and very disturbing descriptions of the pain inflicted by the water torture, see Storey and Codman, *Secretary Root's Record*, 61, 63–64, 65–66.

44. Quoted in Schirmer, *Republic or Empire*, 234.

45. *Manila Times*, November 4, 1901.

46. "The History of Samar," in Storey and Codman, *Secretary Root's Record*, 29–33.

47. Quoted in Stuart Creighton Miller, *Benevolent Assimilation: The American Conquest of the Philippines* (New Haven, CT: Yale University Press, 1982), 81.

48. An excellent study of role of the Macabebes in helping to end the rebellion in the Philippines against the United States is Dennis Edward Flake, *Loyal Macabebes: How the Americans Used the Macabebe Scouts in the Annexation of the Philippines* (Angeles City, Philippines: Holy Angel University Press, 2009).

49. R. F. Pettigrew, quoted in Gamaliel Bradford, letter to the editor, *Springfield Daily Republican*, February 9, 1901.

50. Schirmer, *Republic or Empire*, 227.

51. On the anti-imperialists, see Robert L. Beisner, *Twelve against Empire: The Anti-Imperialists, 1898–1900* (New York: McGraw-Hill, 1968).

52. Mark Twain, "To the Person Sitting in Darkness," *North American Review* 172 (February 1901): 161–76.

53. Quoted in Beisner, *Twelve against Empire*, 175.

54. William Vaughn Moody, "An Ode in Time of Hesitation," in *The Columbia Book of War Poetry*, ed. Richard Marius, http://www.books.google .com=PA133&dq=Lies.

55. "Political Party Platforms, 1840–2012: Republican Party Platform of 1900," American Presidency Project, June 19, 1900, http://www .presidency.ucsb.edu/ws/?pid+29630.

56. Jones, *Honor in the Dust*, 192–93.

57. *Boston Evening Transcript*, February 20, 1902.

58. Schirmer, *Republic or Empire*, 237–38.

59. Jones, *Honor in the Dust*, 277.

60. For another example of administration efforts to excuse American atrocities by citing abuses by Filipinos, see "Mr. Root's Charges against the Filipinos," in Storey and Codman, *Secretary Root's Record*, 53–54.

61. Address of Theodore Roosevelt at Arlington, Memorial Day, May 30, 1902, in Alfred Henry Lewis, ed., *A Compilation of the Messages and Speeches of Theodore Roosevelt, 1901–1905* (New York: Bureau of National Literature and Art, 1906), 28–34.

62. Beisner, *Twelve against Empire*, 153.

63. See John Gates, "The Pacification of the Philippines," chap. 3 in *The US Army and Irregular Warfare*, http://www3.wooster.edu/history/gates/book-ch3.html.

64. George F. Kennan, *American Diplomacy*, 60th anniversary ed. (Chicago: University of Chicago Press, 1984), 21.

65. Quoted in I. V. Lukoinov, "The Portsmouth Peace," in Steven Ericson and Allen Hockley, eds., *The Treaty of Portsmouth and Its Legacies* (Hanover, NH: Dartmouth College Press, 2008), 42.

66. Quoted in John Toland, *The Rising Sun* (New York: Random House, 1970), 169.

67. Quoted in Charles E. Neu, *An Uncertain Friendship: Theodore Roosevelt and Japan, 1906–1909* (Cambridge, MA: Harvard University Press, 1967), 37.

68. Quoted in Toland, *Rising Sun*, 69–70.

69. Theodore Roosevelt, in a letter to William Howard Taft, August 21, 1907, quoted in Neu, *Uncertain Friendship*, 142–43.

70. Quoted in Edmund Morris, *Theodore Rex* (New York: Random House, 2001), 494.

71. Roosevelt to Taft, August 21, 1907, quoted in Neu, *Uncertain Friendship*, 142.

CHAPTER 4: COLD WAR PRELUDE

1. The name of Orwell's article was "You and the Atomic Bomb," and it was published in the *New York Tribune* on October 19, 1945.

2. For a good, recent account of the Cold War, see John Lewis Gaddis, *The Cold War: A New History* (New York: Penguin Press, 2005). Older but still very insightful about the early years of the Cold War is John Lukacs, *A History of the Cold War* (Garden City, NY: Doubleday, 1961).

3. Harry S. Truman, quoted in David McCullough, *Truman* (New York: Simon and Schuster, 1992), 352–53.

4. Harry S. Truman, quoted in ibid., 376. McCullough adds that Charles Bohlen, Truman's advisor for Soviet affairs and later US Ambassador to the Soviet Union, who was present at the interview with Molotov, reported only that Truman dismissed Molotov curtly. Whatever happened that day, Truman's tone was harsh and undiplomatic and very different from the smooth style for which his predecessor, Franklin Roosevelt, was known.

5. Walter Lippmann, in a letter to D. S. Freeman, May 22, 1946.

6. George Kennan (Mr. X), "The Sources of Soviet Conduct," *Foreign Affairs* 25 (July 1947): 566–82.

7. McCullough, *Truman*, 491, 543.

8. Kennan, "Sources of Soviet Conduct."

9. Walter Lippmann, quoted in Ronald Steel, *Walter Lippmann and the American Century* (Boston: Little, Brown, 1980), 444.

10. Walter Lippmann, quoted in ibid.

11. Walter Lippmann, *The Cold War* (New York: Harper and Brothers, 1947).

12. Dwight D. Eisenhower, quoted in Jean Edward Smith, *Eisenhower in War and Peace* (New York: Random House, 2012), 611.

13. Harry S. Truman, *Memoirs by Harry S. Truman*, 2 vols. (Garden City, NY: Doubleday, 1956), 2:91.

14. See John Gittings, "What If Mao Had Met Roosevelt," in *President Gore . . . and Other Things That Did Never Happen*, ed. Duncan Brack (London: Politico's, 2006), 171–83.

15. Jeff Blackwell, "'The China Lobby': Influences on US-China Foreign Policy in the Post War Period, 1949–1954," *Forum* 2 (April 2010): 43–58. See also Ross Y. Koen, *The China Lobby in American Politics* (New York: Harper and Row, 1974).

16. See Nancy Bernhard, *US Television News and Cold War Propaganda,*

1947–1950 (Cambridge, MA: University of Cambridge Press, 1999); and
Thomas Doherty, *Cold War, Cool Medium: Television, McCarthyism, and
American Culture* (New York: Columbia University Press, 2003).

17. Bruce Cummings, *The Korean War: A History* (New York: Modern
Library, 2011), 106.

18. George Kennan, *Memoirs, 1950–1963* (New York: Pantheon Books,
1972), 51.

19. Ibid., 50.

20. Truman, *Memoirs*, 2:333.

21. Mao's decision to enter the Korean conflict is analyzed in Hao
Yufan and Zhai Zhihai, "China's Decision to Enter the Korean War:
History Revisited," *China Quarterly* 121 (March 1990): 94–115.

22. McCullough, *Truman*, 820–22.

23. Joseph Martin, quoted in Michael D. Pearlman, *Truman and
MacArthur* (Bloomington, IN: Indiana University Press, 2008), 179.

24. Ibid., 839–55.

25. Quotations are from Marvin Kalb, *The Road to War: Presidential
Commitments Honored and Betrayed* (Washington, DC: Brookings Institution
Press, 2013), 24.

26. Ibid., 25.

27. Quoted in Robert Griffith. *The Politics of Fear: Joseph R. McCarthy
and the Senate* (Amherst, MA: University of Massachusetts Press, 1970), 49.

28. See E. J. Kahn, *The China Hands: America's Foreign Service Officers
and What Befell Them* (New York: Penguin Books, 1975).

29. *New York Times*, December 3, 1954.

CHAPTER 5: THE VIETNAM DECEPTION

1. Quoted in Marvin Kalb, *The Road to War: Presidential Commitments
Honored and Betrayed* (Washington, DC: Brookings Institution Press, 2013), 29.

2. Ibid., 28–29.

3. Alexander Kendrick, *The Wound Within: America in the Vietnam
Years. 1945–1974* (Boston: Little, Brown, 1974), 37; Neil Sheehan, *A Bright
Shining Lie: John Paul Vann and America in Vietnam* (New York: Vintage
Books, 1989), 152.

4. Quoted in Kalb, *Road to War*, 31.

5. Ibid., 34.

6. Dwight D. Eisenhower, "The Row of Dominoes" (presidential press
conference, April 7, 1954), http://www.vietnamwar.net/Eisenhower-2.htm.

7. "Agreement on the Cessation of Hostilities in Viet-Nam," July 20, 1954, Avalon Project, Yale University Law School, http://avalon.law.yale.edu/20th-century/inch001.asp (page inaccessible as of November 30, 2016).

8. Quoted in Kalb, *Road to War*, 227.

9. John F. Kennedy, quoted in Richard Reeves, *President Kennedy: Profile in Power* (New York: Simon and Schuster, 1994), 53.

10. John F. Kennedy, "Inaugural Address" (Washington, DC, January 20, 1961), American Presidency Project, http://www.presidency.ucsb.edu/ws/index.php?pid=8032.

11. Arthur M. Schlesinger Jr., *A Thousand Days: John F. Kennedy in the White House* (Boston: Houghton Mifflin, 1965), 217.

12. Robert S. McNamara, *In Retrospect: The Tragedy and Lessons of Vietnam* (New York: Vintage Books, 1995), 39.

13. Ibid., 32–33.

14. Kalb, *Road to War*, 57–58.

15. Robert Dallek, *An Unfinished Life: John F. Kennedy, 1917–1963* (Boston: Little, Brown, 2003), 166–67.

16. This account of what MacArthur said to President Kennedy is from an article, "LBJ and the Kennedys," by former Kennedy aide and confidant Kenneth O'Donnell, that appeared in *Life* (August 7, 1970): 51.

17. Quoted in "Madame Nhu, Vietnam War Lightning Rod, Dies," *New York Times*, obituary, April 26, 2011.

18. John F. Kennedy, quoted in O'Donnell, "LBJ and the Kennedys," 51–52.

19. John F. Kennedy, transcript of interview by Walter Cronkite, CBS, September 2, 1963, American Presidency Project, http://www.presidency.ucsb.edu/ws/?pid=9388.

20. Lyndon B. Johnson, quoted in Robert Dallek, *Flawed Giant: Lyndon Johnson and His Times, 1961–1973* (New York: Oxford University Press, 1998), 99.

21. Lyndon B. Johnson, quoted in Doris Kearns Goodwin, *Lyndon Johnson and the American Dream* (New York: Harper and Row, 1976), 263.

22. Drew Babb, "LBJ's 1964 Attack Ad 'Daisy' Leaves a Legacy for Modern Campaigns," *Washington Post*, September 5, 2014, https://www.washingtonpost.com/opinions/lbjs-1964-attack-ad-daisy-leaves-a-legacy-for-modern-campaigns/2014/09/05/d00e66b0-33b4-11e4-9e92-0899b306bbea_story.html?utm_term=.f40eac0a9e69.

23. "The War in Vietnam: Escalation Phase," American Presidency Project, http://www.presidency.ucsb.edu/vietnam/timeline.php.

24. Secretary of Defense McNamara later admitted there was no second attack. See McNamara, *In Retrospect*, 128.

25. Bill Moyers, Speech at National Security Archives (Washington, DC, December 9, 2005), Moyers and Company, http://www.billmoyers.com/2014/08/08/the-farther-one-gets-from-power-the-closer-one-gets-to-the-truth/.

26. Robert McNamara, quoted in Eric Alterman, *When Presidents Lie: A History of Official Deception and Its Consequences* (New York: Penguin, 2004), 205.

27. "Gulf of Tonkin Resolution," The Vietnam War, http://www.vietnamawbb.weebly.com/tonkin-Gulf-resolution.html.

28. McNamara, *In Retrospect*, 120.

29. Ibid., 129.

30. Glenn W. LaFantasie, ed., *Foreign Relations of the United States, 1964–1968*, vol. 3 (Washington, DC: US Government Printing Office, 1996), https://history.state.gov/historicaldocuments/frus1964-68v03.

31. McNamara, *In Retrospect*, 174.

32. Richard Helms, Memorandum for the President, Subject: Effects of the Intensified Air War against North Vietnam, August 29, 1967, quoted in McNamara, *In Retrospect*, 292.

33. On the role and influence of the American media during the Vietnam War, see William M. Hammond, *Reporting Vietnam: Media & Military at War* (Lawrence: University Press of Kansas, 1998); and Daniel C. Hallin, *The Uncensored War: The Media and Vietnam* (New York: Oxford University Press, 1986).

34. Lyndon B. Johnson, quoted in Kalb, *Road to War*, 94.

35. Robert McNamara, quoted in ibid.

36. Ibid., 96.

37. Lyndon B. Johnson, Speech on Vietnam (Johns Hopkins University, Baltimore, MD, April 7, 1965), http://www.lbj.utexas/johnson archives.hom/speeches.hom/165047.asp (page inaccessible as of November 30, 2016).

38. Neither Johnson nor his speechwriters coined the term "Nervous Nellies." According to William Safire's *Political Dictionary* (New York: Oxford University Press, 2008), "Nervous Nellie" was first used to describe peace advocate Frank Kellogg during his Senate confirmation hearings as a nominee for ambassador to the United Kingdom. Earlier, as a US senator, Kellogg had been one of the few Republican members of that body to vote in favor of the Versailles Treaty, which would have led to the United States becoming a member of the League of Nations.

39. These quotations may be found in Safire, *Political Dictionary*, 457.

40. Lyndon B. Johnson, Speech on Vietnam (Miller Center, University of Virginia, Charlottesville, VA, September 29, 1967), http://millercenter .org/president/lbjohnson/speeches/speech-4041.

41. Lyndon B. Johnson, quoted in Michael R. Beschloss, *Reaching for Glory: Lyndon Johnson's Secret White House Tapes, 1964–1965* (New York: Simon and Schuster, 2002), 213.

42. Lyndon B. Johnson, quoted in Kalb, *Road to War*, 90.

43. Lyndon B. Johnson, "Voting Rights Act Address" (Washington, DC, March 15, 1965), Great American Documents, http://www.great americandocuments.com/speeches/lbj-voting-rights.html.

44. J. William Fulbright, *The Arrogance of Power* (New York: Vintage Books, 1966), 182–83.

45. George Kennan, quoted in Vietnam Hearings, January 24, 1966, United States Senate http://www.Senate.gov/artandhistory/history/ minute/Vietnam_Hearings.html.

46. Dallek, *Flawed Giant*, 352.

47. Ibid., 352, 371.

48. Eric Goldman, *The Tragedy of Lyndon Johnson* (New York: Alfred A. Knopf, 1969), 500.

49. Lyndon B. Johnson, quoted in Dallek, *Flawed Giant*, 35.

50. Lyndon B. Johnson, quoted in ibid., 447.

51. Ibid., 390, 449.

52. Ibid., 368–69, 475.

53. See Michael B. Friedland, *Lift Up Your Voice Like a Trumpet: White Clergy and the Civil Rights and Antiwar Movements* (Chapel Hill: University of North Carolina Press, 1998); Benjamin T. Harrison, "Roots of the Anti-Vietnam War Movement," in *The Vietnam Anti-War Movement*, ed. Walter Hickson (New York: Garland, 2000), 99–111; Mary Susannah Robbins, *Against the War in Vietnam: Writings by Activists* (Lanham, MA: Rowman and Littlefield, 2007).

54. Martin Luther King Jr., "Beyond Vietnam" (speech, Riverside Church, New York, April 4, 1967), http://kingencyclopedia.stanford.edu/ encyclopedia/documentsentry/doc_beyond_vietnam/.

55. Lyndon B. Johnson, quoted in Dallek, *Flawed Giant*, 488–89.

56. Hallin, *Uncensored War*, 106.

57. "Final Words: Cronkite's Vietnam Commentary," *All Things Considered*, NPR, July 18, 2009, http://www.npr.org/templates/story/story .php?storyId=1067756.

CHAPTER 6: THE DEFEATED GIANT

1. Richard Nixon, quoted in Richard Reeves, *President Nixon: Alone in the White House* (New York: Simon and Schuster, 2001), 439–40.

2. Quoted in Seymour M. Hersh, *My Lai 4: A Report on the Massacre and Its Aftermath* (New York: Random House, 1970), 42.

3. See W. R. Peers, *The My Lai Inquiry* (New York: W. W. Norton, 1979), 91. Peers was a lieutenant general placed in charge of the actual My Lai inquest.

4. *Manila Times*, November 4, 1901.

5. Quoted in Karen D. Smith, "American Soldiers Testify in My Lai Court Martial," *Amarillo Globe-News*, December 6, 2000, http://amarillo .com/stories/2000/12/06/fri_120600-36.shtml#.V8hs4fkrK1s.

6. Quoted in Seymour M. Hersh, "Eyewitness Accounts of the My Lai Massacre," *Cleveland Plain Dealer*, November 20, 1969.

7. For Thompson's testimony, see Peers, *My Lai Inquiry*, 66–67.

8. For a study of the parallels between the Nuremberg and My Lai trials, see Jay Baird, ed., *From Nuremberg to My Lai* (Lexington, MA: D. C. Heath, 1972).

9. These Calley quotations are from *Lieutenant Calley: His Own Story*, as told to John Stack (New York: Viking Press, 1971), 80–85, 95–121.

10. Jay Baird, *From Nuremberg to My Lai*, 213.

11. Nick Turse, *Kill Anything That Moves: The Real American War and Vietnam* (New York: Picador, 2013).

12. Ibid., 8, 21.

13. Ibid., 42.

14. Ibid., 49.

15. Marvin Kalb, *The Road to War: Presidential Commitments Honored and Betrayed* (Washington, DC: Brookings Institution Press, 2013), 153.

16. Richard Nixon, in *Foreign Relations of the United States*, ed. Department of State Office of the Historian (Washington, DC: US Government Publishing Office, 2006), 14:434.

17. Richard M. Nixon, "Address to the Nation on the Situation in Southeast Asia" (Washington, DC, April 30, 1970), American Presidency Project, http://www.presidency.ucsb.edu/ws/?pid=2490.

18. Ibid.

19. Quoted in Evan Thomas, *Being Nixon: A Man Divided* (New York: Random House, 2015), p. 267.

20. See Charles Hirschman, Samuel Preston, and Vu Manh Loi,

"Vietnamese Casualties during the American War," *Population and Development Review* (December 1995): 783–812.

21. Gerald R. Ford, Address at Tulane University (New Orleans, LA, April 23, 1975), American Presidency Project, http://www.presidency .ucsb.edu/ws/?pid=4859.

CHAPTER 7: UNRAVELING IRAQ

1. Jean Edward Smith, *Bush* (New York: Simon and Schuster, 2016), 279.

2. Ibid., 169.

3. Peter Baker, *Days of Fire: Bush and Cheney in the White House* (New York: Doubleday, 2013), 230–31.

4. On neoconservatism, see Stefan Halper and Jonathan Clarke, *America Alone: The Neo-Conservatives and the Global Order* (New York: Cambridge University Press, 2004); and Irwin Stelzer, ed., *Neoconservatism* (London: Atlantic Books, 2004).

5. George W. Bush, transcript of debate excerpts, *PBS NewsHour*, October 12, 2000, http://www.pbs.org/newshour/bb/politics-july-dec00 -for-policy_10-12/ (accessed November 30, 2016); "Presidential Debates: 1960 and 1976–2016," *American Presidency Project*, http://www.presidency .ucsb.edu/ws/?pid=29419 (accessed November 30, 2016).

6. George W. Bush, quoted in Robert Draper, *Dead Certain: The Presidency of George W. Bush* (New York: Simon and Schuster, 200732.

7. George W. Bush, quoted in Jacob Weisberg, *The Bush Tragedy* (New York: Random House, 2008), 63.

8. See Margaret Garrard Warner, "Bush Battles the 'Wimp Factor,'" *Newsweek*, October 19, 1987.

9. Donald Rumsfeld, quoted in Baker, *Days of Fire*, 91.

10. George W. Bush, "Address to the Nation on the September 11 Attacks," in *Selected Speeches of George W. Bush, 2001–2008*, 57–58, http:// georgewbush-whitehouse.archives.gov/infocus/bushrecord/documents/ Selected_Speeches_George_W_Bush.pdf.

11. Tom Daschle, quoted in Baker, *Days of Fire*, 135.

12. George W. Bush, Second State of the Union Address (Washington, DC, January 29, 2002), https://georgewbush-whitehouse.archives.gov/ news/releases/2002/01/20020129-11.html.

13. See Bob Woodward, *Plan of Attack* (New York: Simon and Schuster, 2004), 86–92.

14. Michael Isikoff and David Corn, *Hubris: The Inside Story of Spin, Scandal, and the Selling of the Iraq War* (New York: Three Rivers Press, 2007), 1.

15. See, for example, Stephen Richter, "Reverse Domino Theory: George W. Bush Applying the 'Domino Theory' to the Countries of the Middle East?" *Globalist*, February 20, 2003, http://www.theglobalist.com/reverse-domino-theory/.

16. See Shao-chuan Lang, ed., *Coping with Crises: How Governments Deal with Crises*, 10 vols. (Lanham, MD: University Press of America, 1990), 2:175–76.

17. Richard "Dick" Cheney, in transcript of *Meet the Press*, NBC, September 14, 2002, http://www.nbcnews.com/id/3080244/ns/meet_the_press/t/transcript-sept/.

18. Richard Clarke, quoted in Baker, *Days of Fire*, 135.

19. Joint Resolution, 107th Cong., Public Law 40, September 18, 2001, US Government Printing Office.

20. Baker, *Days of Fire*, 144.

21. Ibid., 145.

22. Isikoff and Corn, *Hubris*, 3–6.

23. Ibid., 89.

24. Ibid., 102–105; National Commission on Terrorist Attacks upon the United States, Thomas H. Kean, and Lee Hamilton. *The 9/11 Commission Report: Final Report of the National Commission on Terrorist Attacks upon the United States* (Washington, DC: National Commission on Terrorist Attacks upon the United States, 2004), 229.

25. Richard "Dick" Cheney, in transcript of *Meet the Press*, NBC, September 10, 2006, http://www.nbcnews.com/id/14720480/ns/meet_the_press/t/transcript-sept/#.V8hz5vkrK1s.

26. Isikoff and Corn, *Hubris*, 66–152.

27. US Congress, Senate, Select Committee on Intelligence, September 8, 2006, 106–108.

28. George W. Bush, State of the Union Address, January 29, 2002.

29. Richard "Dick" Cheney, in transcript of *Meet the Press*, NBC, March 16, 2003, http://www.nbcnews.com/id/3080244/ns/meet_the_press/t/transcript-sept/.

30. Condoleezza Rice, transcript of interview by Wolf Blitzer, *CNN Late Edition*, September 8, 2002, http://www.cnn.com/TRANSCRIPTS/0209/08/le.00.html.

31. Condoleezza Rice, transcript of interview by Margaret Warner, *PBS NewsHour*, September 25, 2002, http://www.pbs.org/newshour/bb/international-july-dec02-rice_9-25/.

32. Wolf Blitzer, "Search for the 'Smoking Gun,'" *CNN*, January 10, 2003, http://www.cnn.com/2003/US/01/10/wbr.smoking.gun/.

33. Colin Powell, *It Worked for Me: In Life and Leadership* (New York: HarperCollins, 2012), 210.

34. Ibid., 210–11.

35. Brent Scowcroft, "Don't Attack Iraq," *New York Times*, October 15, 2002.

36. See Jon Meacham, *Destiny and Power: The American Odyssey of George Herbert Walker Bush* (New York: Random House, 2015), 570.

37. George W. Bush, quoted in ibid., 571.

38. George W. Bush, quoted in Woodward, *Plan of Attack*, 421.

39. Quoted in Meacham, *Destiny and Power*, 572.

40. George H. W. Bush, quoted in ibid., 588.

41. George H. W. Bush, quoted in ibid., 589.

42. Malcolm Byrne, "State Department Experts Warned CENTCOM before Iraq War about Lack of Plans for Post-War Iraq Security," *Electronic Briefing Book No. 163*, National Security Archive, August 17, 2005, http://nsarchive.gwu.edu/NSAEBB/NSAEBB163/.

43. Isikoff and Corn, *Hubris*, 137, 296, 414.

44. See Steven Kull, Clay Ramsey, and Evan Lewis, "Misperceptions, the Media, and the Iraq War," *Political Science Quarterly* 118 (Winter 2003): 569–98; Anup Shah, "Iraq War Media Reporting, Journalism and Propaganda," *Global Issues*, August 1, 2007.

45. Isikoff and Corn, *Hubris*, 60.

46. *New York Times*, May 26, 2004.

47. Isikoff and Corn, *Hubris*, 186.

48. Powell, *It Worked for Me*, 222–23.

49. George W. Bush, "The Future of Iraq" (speech to American Enterprise Institute, Washington, DC, February 26, 2003), Presidential Rhetoric, http://www.Presidentialrhetoric.com/speeches/02.26.03.html.

50. Isikoff and Corn, *Hubris*, 25.

51. Quoted in Smith, *Bush*, 226.

52. Quoted in ibid., 339.

53. George W. Bush, *Decision Points* (New York: Crown, 2010), 396–97. See also National Security Strategy of the United States, September 17, 2002, http://www.state.gov/documents/organization/63562.pdf; "The Bush Doctrine," *New York Times*, September 22, 2002.

54. See Henry Shue and David Rodin, *Preemption: Military Action and Moral Justification* (Oxford: Oxford University Press, 2007).

55. Robert McFadden, "From New York to Melbourne, Protests against War on Iraq," *New York Times*, February 16, 2003; Ishaan Tharoor, "Viewpoint: Why Was the Biggest Protest in History Ignored?" *Time*, February 15, 2013.

56. For a succinct description and analyses of the Iraq Inquiry, see "Report Outlines Flaws of Britain's Path to War," *New York Times*, July 7, 2016.

57. Michael B. Kelley and Geoffrey Ingersoll, "The Staggering Cost of the Last Decade's War in Iraq—In Numbers," *Business Insider*, June 20, 2014. See also "Iraq Study Estimates War-Related Deaths at 461,000," *BBC News*, October 16, 2013, http://www.bbc.com/world-middle-east-24547256.

58. Sean Loughlin, "Rumsfeld on Looting in Iraq," *CNN Washington Bureau*, April 12, 2003, http://www.cnn.com/2003/US/o4/11/sprj.irq.pentagon/.

59. Donald Rumsfeld, quoted in David Corn and Siddhartha Mahanta, "Rumsfeld's Memoir," *Mother Jones*, February 8, 2011.

60. *Le Monde*, September 12, 2001.

61. Richard "Dick" Cheney, quoted in Dana Milbank and Spencer Hsu, "Cheney: Kerry Victory is Risky," *Washington Post*, September 8, 2004.

62. George W. Bush, "Second Inaugural Address" (speech, Washington, DC, January 20, 2005), Avalon Project: The Inaugural Addresses of the Presidents, http://avalon.law.yale.edu/21st_century/gbush2.asp.

63. George W. Bush, transcript of debate excerpts, *PBS NewsHour*, October 12, 2000, http://www.pbs.org/newshour/bb/politics-july-dec00-for-policy_10-12.

64. Baker, *Days of Fire*, 457.

65. *New York Times*, December 8, 2015.

66. Seymour M. Hersh, "Torture at Abu Ghraib," *New Yorker*, May 10, 2004.

67. Antonio M. Taguba, quoted in ibid.

68. Ibid.

69. Ibid.

70. The full text of the Taguba Report may be found on *FindLaw*: http://news.findlaw.com/cnn/docs/iraq/tagubarpt.html.

71. Quoted in Thomas E. Ricks, *Fiasco: The American Military Adventure in Iraq, 2003–2005* (New York: Penguin Books, 2007), 197.

72. On the connections between the American invasion of Iraq and the rise of the Islamic State, see Phyllis Bennis, *Understanding ISIS and the New Global War on Terror* (Northampton, MA: Interlink, 2015), 16–23.

INDEX